CH

Hip Ideas for Hyper Dogs

AMY AMMEN

AND

KITTY FOTH-REGNER

BICENTENNIAL
1807
⊛WILEY
2007
BICENTENNIAL

MAR 07

Wiley Publishing, Inc.

Copyright © 2007 by Wiley Publishing, Inc., Hoboken, New Jersey. All rights reserved.

Howell Book House
Published by Wiley Publishing, Inc., Hoboken, New Jersey

For general information on our other products and services or to obtain technical support please contact our Customer Care Department within the U.S. at (800) 762-2974, outside the U.S. at (317) 572-3993 or fax (317) 572-4002.

Wiley also publishes its books in a variety of electronic formats. Some content that appears in print may not be available in electronic books. For more information about Wiley products, please visit our web site at www.wiley.com.

Library of Congress Cataloging-in-Publication Data:
Ammen, Amy.
  Hip ideas for hyper dogs / Amy Ammen and Kitty Foth-Regner.
     p. cm.
  Includes index.
  ISBN 978-0-470-04101-7 (pbk. : alk. paper)
  1. Dogs—Training. 2. Dogs—Behavior. I. Foth, Kitty. II. Title.
  SF431.A437 2007
  636.7'0835—dc22

                         2006025511

Printed in the United States of America

10 9 8 7 6 5 4 3 2 1

Book design by Erin Zeltner
Cover design by Wendy Mount
Book production by Wiley Publishing, Inc. Composition Services

To Amy's Dad, for two inspiring examples of when and why to follow one's instincts.

And Kitty's husband, Dave, for never once complaining about the evenings and weekends lost to working on this book.

Also by Amy Ammen from Howell Book House:

Training in No Time: An Expert's Approach to Effective Dog Training for Hectic Lifestyles

Dog Training: An Owner's Guide to a Happy Healthy Pet

Contents

··

Acknowledgments

A thousand thanks to all those who helped make this book a reality, including:

Wiley Publishing acquisitions editor Pam Mourouzis for sharing our vision

Editor Beth Adelman for her outstanding suggestions on improving our manuscript

Photographers Wendy Simon, Jan Plagenz, James Weyenberg, and Donna Krischan

Beth Castro, who provided us with a perfect location for our biggest photo shoot

Lynette Bartelt and Todd Thurber, who provided both human and canine talent for that photo shoot

Two dozen other dog fanciers who contributed their expertise or photos or both, from as far away as England and Greece

The many Amiable Dog Training students who gave us insight into the inner workings of their own hyper dogs

Amiable office manager Mary Ebel, whose competence and attention to detail allowed Amy to give her full attention to this book

Each other, for making our working Mondays the best day of the week

And Able, Obey, The Beaver, Shadow, and Lucy, for keeping us laughing during even the most grueling days

Index of Basic Skills

∙∙∙

To train a hyper dog, we teach ourselves and our dogs a handful of basic commands, techniques, and skills. Then we apply them in different combinations to achieve reliable one-command control. Here's where you'll find the most detailed explanations of the key skills and techniques in this book—the ones we refer to again and again.

Introduction

···

Welcome to the world of the hyperactive dog! If you're looking at this book, chances are you're already experiencing the joys and trials of owning one of these incredible creatures.

There's nothing unusual about your situation. It seems that hyper dogs are more common today than ever before, perhaps because of breed choices, perhaps because most of us are too busy to spend as much time with our dogs as we used to, perhaps a combination of these factors and others.

Whatever the reason, we see hyper dogs everywhere these days—pulling, panting, leaping, growling, pacing, barking, busy as beavers, and causing their owners absolute fits.

It seems no one is immune. My coauthor, for instance, lives with three hyper dogs, and they've all learned a great deal as we developed this book.

In fact, her experience is one of the reasons the two of us got to talking about hyper dogs in the first place. We found that there was a dearth of valid information to help the beleaguered dog owner deal with these sometimes monstrous critters—and even less on how to transform them into mild-mannered versions of themselves, especially for busy owners who find themselves in a constant time crunch.

THERE'S NO REASON TO DESPAIR

My own experience with hyper dogs began when I was 11 and lived with my family in the country northwest of Milwaukee, Wisconsin. After listening to my pestering for almost a year, my father finally agreed to let me have a dog—on the condition that he or she would live outside.

And so I bought my first dog—a 4-month old, puppy-mill-bred Siberian Husky I named Tess. What a rush it was at first, having my own puppy! But then reality set in. She didn't listen to me. She didn't obey. She was, I have to admit, completely out of control.

1

It took me nearly a year to figure out how to get and keep her attention and persuade her to follow my will rather than her own. Once we'd reached that milestone, life with Tess was terrific. Naturally, I then jumped to the obvious conclusion: If having one dog made the world more delightful than ever before, how fantastic would it be to have two?

My dad didn't put up much of a fight this time. Soon I came home with Huzzi, a 5-month-old Australian Cattle Dog, and a new life goal: making mine the best-behaved, best-conditioned, and best-loved dogs in all the world.

My dad was the obvious inspiration for this resolve. I wanted to prove to him that letting me get a second dog was a brilliant call. But there was a more subtle motivator at work, as well—a motivator based solely on what others thought of me.

You see, even 30 years ago, people were repelled by the notion of a dog being banished from the house. Even though both Huskies and Cattle Dogs have been bred to thrive in climates harsher than southeast Wisconsin's, I couldn't shake the feeling that people were frowning on what might seem to be inhumane living conditions—and, of course, on *me* as the person who was responsible.

As a result, when I wasn't at school or working at my part-time kennel helper/apprentice groomer job, I was working with Tess and Huzzi. I spent tons of time bonding with them. I carefully socialized them with other animals as well as with humans. I conditioned them painstakingly. I examined them thoroughly and regularly, checking their eyes, ears, mouth, feet, legs, and bodies for any signs of disease or injury. And I groomed them religiously. All these tasks were easy, because I'd adapted standard training techniques and applied them consistently to all our interactions. As a result, these dogs were truly a delight to be around.

My efforts paid off: A couple years later, my dad admitted that yet another dog couldn't hurt. And soon Tess and Huzzi were joined by a Briard named Weaselle.

This combination might have been a recipe for disaster. Each of these three breeds has a well-deserved reputation for being difficult to work with. And, as many chagrined former owners will testify, Huskies, Australian Cattle Dogs, and Briards can be the epitome of the overly exuberant canine: intensely energetic, wickedly smart, often rebellious, and potentially dominating or even aggressive. But no disaster was forthcoming. My success with Tess and Huzzi had taught me how to appreciate and draw out every last ounce of potential these dogs possessed.

The canine companions who taught me how to train dogs were (left to right) Siberian Husky Tess, UD, Australian Cattle Dog Huzzi, UD, and Briard Ch. Weaselle, UD.

I was *very* proud of them. Not only did they bring home consistent wins in the obedience trials we began entering, they turned into the best companions imaginable. The four of us enjoyed a truly easy, symbiotic relationship.

Eventually, I opened my own school, Amiable Dog Training (www.dogclass.com). And over the last quarter century, tens of thousands of dog owners have benefited from the techniques I teach, learning to build peaceful, easy lives with their dogs. Now it's your turn.

No Time to Spare?

If you're the current owner of a hyper dog, perhaps the best news to emerge from my experience is this: Back in the days of Tess, Huzzi, and Weaselle, my schedule was so crazy that I didn't have a moment to spare. So I was forced to develop training techniques that would deliver these extraordinary results just as quickly as possible.

In short, my techniques are tailor-made for owners who don't have time to fool around. Which means that, by picking up this book, you may officially have run out of excuses for your hyper dog's bad behavior.

Speaking of excuses . . .

Great Expectations

Some people who bring their hyper dogs in for training at Amiable are heavy on excuses and light on expectations.

My dog is very smart, they'll say—or very stubborn or spiteful. Or they might say she needs to grow up and get it out of her system (whatever "it" is). Or they might blame their dog's breed, gender, or size. For instance:

"He runs away because he's a Husky."

"Sure, she nips a little. She protects our family because she's being maternal."

"He barks. What can you expect from a Sheltie?"

"She's a terrier; she's going to go nuts with all these other dogs around."

"Pomeranians have a Napoleon complex."

"All Beagles disobey commands, don't they?"

Such biases are not harmless. On the contrary, they can sabotage your training efforts before you even snap on the leash. After all, if you really believe that Coonhounds are incapable of paying attention to you when they're on the trail of a good scent, you're not likely to master the necessary steps for interrupting yours in the midst of a hunt. If you think a Jack Russell Terrier's histrionics in the presence of other dogs is genetic, you're more likely to avoid those situations than to try to correct your dog's behavior. If you're convinced that your Lhasa Apso's surliness is a reflection of her ancestral role as a sentinel, you may find yourself shooing children away rather than dealing with her bad attitude.

Perhaps these excuses sound familiar to you. Or maybe you've come up with some unique ones of your own. If that's the case, I hope this book will free you to see that they serve no good purpose—and that every creature appreciates having the opportunity to be all that she can be. Even that crazy dog of yours.

FREEDOM FROM FOOD

This book will teach you how to train your hyper dog by using your hands, leash, voice, body language, and precise timing—a combination of reliably fast-acting tools that will produce not only a strong bond between you and your dog, but also a rapid increase in your dog's confidence and your own.

You may have noticed one item that's *not* on this list of tools: treats. That's because problems can arise in dogs trained using food lures. Most notably, in the absence of such lures, they can be unresponsive to commands. That's especially true in the presence of distractions, when it's most critical that dogs heed their owners.

Although food lures *can* be useful in the later, more intricate stages of training, for such activities as freestyle obedience competition, beginning and intermediate trainers are better off without the false sense of security treats can create—and without the subsequent difficulty of weaning their dogs from treat-induced obedience.

Bottom line: This food-free approach to training delivers lasting, dependable results more quickly than any treat-based program ever could—and in the process can help improve your hyper dog's character, often dramatically.

HEALTH AND SAFETY

Hyper dogs can become just as sick, hurt, and out of shape as their more sedentary cousins. And a number of the activities suggested in this book can be physically demanding. For example, up-the-stairs retrieves can be hard on an older dog's joints and bones. So I urge you to check with your veterinarian before engaging in the more strenuous activities presented in this book.

It pays to be safety-conscious, too. While most owners are so afraid of injuring their dogs that they're overly timid with their corrections and requests, occasionally an owner is so fearless that he may put his dog at risk of serious injury.

I've provided specific safety tips when describing any potentially risky activity. But the most important tip I can give you is to work with your dog until you have reliable control over her in just about any situation. In general, don't try anything wilder than long walks and confined retrieving until you've *both* mastered the basic obedience tasks described in chapter 3.

Happy training!

Amy Ammen

Chapter 1

The Hyper Dog

A curse or a blessing?

··

Shaker was the first puppy I brought home after I'd grown up and moved from my parents' house to a place of my own. An American Staffordshire Terrier, she was not beautiful, brilliant, or particularly excited about learning. But she was a decent dog and I was by then an experienced professional trainer. When it came to obedience and household training, we should have had our act together.

Sadly, she was like the shoemaker's barefoot children.

One day, for instance, I was hanging up some clothes in my bedroom when the phone rang. It was a call I'd been waiting for and I raced to answer it, leaving my sweet young Shaker alone in the bedroom.

An hour later, I hung up and went back to my room to finish putting my clothes away—and found every surface in the room, from floor to bed to bureau, covered with white dust. Shaker had discovered my economy-size container of baby powder.

My error was overconfidence, combined with a good dollop of plain old laziness. I'd given her too much freedom too soon.

It took me so long to clean up that mess, you would think I would've learned my lesson. But no: We lived in a rural community, my roommate and I, and when my puppy and her equally adorable baby Labrador Retriever wanted to go outside, it was much easier to open the door and let them out than it was to don jackets and boots and give them a proper escort.

I'm ashamed to admit that, more than once, they took full advantage of their freedom and checked out a neighboring pig farm—coming home only after they'd both enjoyed a good roll in the sty.

These weren't the only incidents. Together or alone, these puppies managed to wreak havoc on our home—making messes, noise, and pests out of themselves, and leaving a path of destruction in their wake.

The Common Denominator: Hyper-dogdom

There was nothing wrong with these puppies. *I* was the problem, especially given my growing experience in counseling exasperated dog owners. I should have known better than to let these little critters run wild.

After all, as puppies they were, by definition, hyper dogs, fun-loving and easily stimulated. And because they were also undertrained, they had no concept of right and wrong; they were totally out of control.

If that sounds familiar, then you already know how very challenging these dogs can be. Perhaps the thought of getting rid of yours has already crossed your mind a time or two; maybe you've even checked out the web site for his breed's rescue group or your local Humane Society, just to see what it would take to find him a more appropriate home.

Hyper or Neurotic?

Is your dog hyper, or is he full-blown neurotic?

Don't answer too quickly. Both hyper and neurotic dogs can exhibit a range of behaviors from merely annoying to bordering on the intolerable. A few common examples:

- Whining
- Barking
- Terrorizing others, from husbands to guests to other pets
- Separation anxiety

In many cases—perhaps most—these behavioral issues can be rectified with the techniques described in this book. But that won't always be the case.

How far you're able to get with your dog will tell you whether he is simply a hyper dog who is ready to become a great companion for you, or a true neurotic who will be a never-ending project.

Generally speaking, the best course of action is to make as much headway as you can on your own, following the suggestions we offer here. When you and your pooch have reached a plateau and you're not yet satisfied with his behavior, it's time to seek professional help.

It's not always smart to wait, though. Occasionally, bad habits can make the dog a threat to himself or to others who happen to cross his path. A dog who licks his legs obsessively, chews holes in his flesh, or bites off the tip of his tail needs to see his veterinarian and also needs appropriate deterrents, comforts, and distractions. One who bites strangers or jumps through windows when Mom leaves the house needs the immediate and intensive professional intervention of an experienced trainer.

But then . . . you watch your dog sleeping peacefully and get a glimpse once again of the beautiful companion you imagined when you brought him home. Or you tell him to sit or lie down or come, and—miracle of miracles—he does, and you know that you've just witnessed a flash of the brilliance that could one day make this pooch the very best thing that has ever happened to you. Or (admit it!) you picture yourself saying goodbye as you hand him over to his new owner, and your heart begins to break.

My Shaker was a perfect example of a dog whose potential was hidden beneath a veneer of naughtiness. But once I started training her, she not only became a splendid companion, she also became one of America's top-ranked obedience terriers and was the first American Staffordshire Terrier to have earned AKC Champion and Obedience Trial Champion titles.

So if your dog's behavior has you just about at your wit's end, don't throw in the towel. Instead, get ready to harness the potential of your hyperactive canine work-in-progress.

REAP THE REWARDS

Just about every hyper dog seems to have too much of what we ordinarily consider a very good thing: energy! In fact, most of us would like to have a little more of that elusive quality.

Still, smart dog owners don't lament this fact of hyper-canine life. Instead, they learn to harness and redirect all that energy. And in the process, they reap substantial rewards.

Physical Health

When your dog has more energy than you do, you'll have to find some mutually acceptable way of dissipating his. The good news is that in the process you'll probably find that you've picked up some extra energy. You may even find that working with your high-energy dog burns off extra calories and gets you in shape even more reliably and pleasurably than a membership at an expensive fitness center ever could.

Katherine Koetting is a great example of a handler whose association with a hyper dog has led to greatly enhanced health. She showed up at Amiable Dog Training's Brookfield studio one Wednesday night with a 10-year-old German Shepherd–Doberman Pinscher mix named Brandy.

Brandy wasn't hers; she belonged to Katherine's neighbors. Interested in getting some exercise for herself, for 18 months Katherine had been walking the dog every day. Their walks were uneventful—unless they happened to run into certain dogs along the way. Then, Brandy showed her aggressive side, barking, lunging, and generally demonstrating her eagerness to get into a fight.

Katherine could easily have given up on Brandy, but she knew that without this canine incentive, she'd also give up on her own exercise.

At first, she tried managing the situation by changing the time of their walks, by altering their route, and by crossing her fingers. But there was never a guarantee that they wouldn't run into another "unacceptable" dog.

Finally, Katherine decided to give training a whirl. It worked: Basic obedience training has enabled her to take charge of the situation. What was once an almost daily ordeal has become pleasurable for woman and dog alike. And Katherine has already lost a full dress size without changing her diet one bit.

Her experience is not at all surprising. Over the years, dozens of my students have reported losing significant amounts of weight—including pounds that had stubbornly resisted all their previous efforts at dieting.

This effect has not gone unnoticed by the medical community. For instance, researchers at the University of Missouri-Columbia recently followed the progress of a group of people who added dog-walking to their daily routines. The participants lost an average of 14 pounds each over the course of a year—more than the average loss reported by major weight-loss programs.

Mental Health

Perhaps even more important, working with a hyper dog can do wonders for your attitude toward life. One reason is laughter. It's pretty difficult to keep a straight face when you're watching a dog tearing around the backyard, his back end tucked in and an expression on his face that can only be described as a grin. And, truth be told, hyper dogs sometimes get themselves in situations that are impossibly funny—even if they *have* made a mess of things.

But that's hardly a hyper dog's only contribution to your mental health. Consider what he can do for your self-esteem. The ability to give unconditional love seems to be part of any dog's genetic footprint, but hyper dogs are poised to deliver new levels of affection and devotion if you'll only give them the chance.

Hyper dogs can also put your mind to work; you have to be clever to stay one step ahead of a super-energetic canine. In fact, a very wise owner once told me that training her dog did more for her mental sharpness than working the *New York Times* crossword puzzle. I have to agree. Helping a dog reach his full potential takes careful preparation, planning, implementation, and follow-through.

Some years ago, I visited my friend Gail, a great hostess who set plates of beautiful hors d'oeuvres out on her coffee table almost before I had a chance to sit down. I wasn't the only one who noticed, though. Australian Shepherd Chelsea hovered nearby, just waiting for her chance to sample her mistress's work.

She didn't get that opportunity, because Gail kept an eye on her and delivered continual warnings and threats. But Gail could have made it much easier on herself by preparing for the situation. If she had attached a leash to Chelsea's collar before setting out the food, she could have given the leash a quick jerk the moment the dog wiggled her nostrils—and that would probably have been the end of the issue.

What I've just described is a standard correction that simply requires planning ahead. But there may be times when a standard approach doesn't work on your hyper dog and you'll have to put on your thinking cap.

Sometimes a dog's background or breed can be a factor. For example, it can be difficult to teach a Greyhound to sit on command. When you try to use the normal pull up/push down technique, you encounter amazing resistance. It's not that he's being defiant; Greyhounds (as well as a few other breeds, including Dachshunds and Dobermans) just tend to lock their legs when they stand. It took a little thought to come up with a solution for this idiosyncrasy: Quickly walk the dog forward several steps while using your hands to fold him into the sit position.

Out-of-the-ordinary situations can also arise with a hyper dog, challenging your ability to quickly think your way to a solution. Not long ago, I was working with a moderately trained dog on a light line in a busy park, only to have the line somehow slip off his collar. My temptation, of course, was to run after the dog in a panic. Instead, I caught his attention for a split second by barking out, "Hey!" At the same time, I bent down to grasp an imaginary line and ran away saying, "Good, good, *good!*" It worked; the dog responded as if he and I were still securely attached to one another.

The need for great timing, as you monitor your dog's every glance and twitch, will also help keep you sharp. If he's even thinking about getting into some mischief or losing control of his emotions, a timely intervention can have a profound effect. It will not only nip this particular episode in the bud, but it can also keep him from going there the next time this particular combination of stimuli arises.

Social Health

A highly energetic dog can also help you make new friends. He's usually friendlier than calm dogs and more eager to introduce himself to strangers. And his antics can attract the attention of passersby. In some neighborhoods, this attention can qualify you instantly and automatically for membership in the local canine social circle.

An outgoing dog can also play Cupid. Not long ago, one of my girlfriends was walking her 85-pound female black Lab when she spotted a very attractive man coming around the corner. The dog didn't hesitate; she made a dash for him, yanking the leash right out of my friend's hand and greeting the fellow with great enthusiasm. He was new to town, they were both available, and they've been dating ever since.

A Healthier Home

Finally, the best motivation for keeping your house neat and your valuables put away has four legs. There's nothing like a hyper dog to force you to pick up your shoes and socks, put your laundry in the hamper, take out the trash, and keep everything from treasured books to disposable writing instruments tucked away, safely out of reach.

And it's an effort that requires constant vigilance. Happily for our homes, we can't afford to let our guard down no matter how well-trained our hyper dogs are.

I learned that lesson well with my treasured Chihuahua mix, Able—an amazing dog who is my constant companion and is my formal dance partner at events like the Wisconsin State Fair. This dog is well trained and willing—surely safe in any circumstance, right?

Wrong. A few years ago, I left the door to my walk-in closet cracked open and Able let himself in. I discovered him gnawing at the heel of a Via Spiga shoe carelessly left on the floor.

Fortunately for Able, a prospective employee phoned just as I caught him in the act. So he was spared my misdirected retribution. At the same time, he taught me an important lesson: No dog is ever 100 percent foolproof, and it's best to keep valuables out of his reach. A corollary: When you do let down your guard and your dog takes advantage of the opportunity, don't be too harsh on him; after all, dogs will be dogs no matter how well trained they may be. In the expensive lesson of the Via Spiga, I was the one at fault—not Able.

Chapter 2

The Personality Profile

What type of hyper dog do you have?

···

S ome breeds seem to have earned a special place in the chronicles of hyper-dogdom. Irish Setters, Wheaton Terriers, and Border Collies are just three examples of dogs with loads of personality and an extra dose of excitability to match. Others have earned the reputation of being laid-back. You don't expect to see a Clumber Spaniel, Dandie Dinmont Terrier, or Irish Wolfhound bouncing off the walls.

But there are always exceptions, and generalizing is as useless in canines as it is in humans. There can be wide variations within each breed, even among littermates.

The fact is, the out-of-control doggie hall of fame is populated by everything from hyper hounds to torrid terriers to take-charge toys. If you've been blessed with one of these creatures, the only sensible course of action is to treat and train your dog as the individual that she is.

So where do you begin?

SIZING UP YOUR DOG

Whether you have a purebred, a mutt, or a representative of today's increasingly popular "designer breeds"—a Puggle or a Schnoodle, say—size is as good a place as any to start. That's because some traits and techniques are especially relevant to dogs of certain dimensions.

Small Dogs

- American Eskimo Dog
- Beagle

- Bichon Frise
- Boston Terrier
- Chihuahua
- Dachshund
- Jack Russell Terrier
- Maltese
- Miniature Pinscher
- Miniature Schnauzer
- Pomeranian
- Poodle (Miniature and Toy)
- Pug
- Rat Terrier
- Shih Tzu
- Toy Fox Terrier
- Yorkshire Terrier

When a dog is both little and hyper, her small stature and her owner's desire to coddle and protect her can be a dangerous combination. It's understandable: We may be so afraid of injuring our little pooches that we underdirect and spoil them, making greater allowances for ill manners just because they're so cute.

We may refuse to put collars on them for fear of damaging their delicate tracheas, or balk at pushing them into the sit position for fear of injuring their spines or legs. We may freak out if they become excited and start reverse sneezing—a noisy but totally benign action. We may become frantic if they begin quivering even when they aren't scared, cold, or in pain, and wind up giving them sympathy that only encourages repeat performances in the future.

We may overcompensate for a slipped stifle, calling it quits on training rather than simply letting the dog walk it out. We may insist on picking our pooch up whenever another dog or a toddler expresses interest in her.

And do we make our little dogs move when they're in our way? Never! We'd much rather go out of *our* way to avoid the possibility of injuring or frightening our precious pooches.

The trouble is, none of this is necessary and none of it is conducive to having a well-behaved dog. In my experience, small dogs are generally no less durable than their medium and large cousins. And while I always recommend tailoring one's approach to training to fit the dog's size, personality, and determination to pursue her own agenda, there are very few dogs who require such extremely delicate handling. If you're in doubt about yours, check with your veterinarian. If you don't, you could be courting disaster, because overly protective, attentive, or sympathetic treatment can make hyper behaviors even more pronounced. Take a sulky dog and spoil her, and she may soon be doing everything from barking and resisting restraint to snarling and even biting. She may even become prone to taking off whenever she has a chance, oblivious to your cries to stop and come back—a truly dangerous turn of events.

I know the temptations associated with small dogs only too well, because I've lived for many years in a high-rise condo in the city and my dogs have all been on the tiny side. From time to time even I have been tempted to break down and pamper one of my little creatures—but as an experienced urban dweller and small-dog owner, I do my best to distinguish behavior that deserves correction from behavior that's benign and truly cute.

My 3.5-pound Chihuahua, Smartie, tested my objectivity countless times. The day I brought her home from the humane society, for instance, my 12-pound male Chihuahua mix, Able, walked over to check her out. Smartie's hackles immediately went up, and she charged him full force. I thought it was good that she was holding her ground. And it was actually kind of cute, this tiny dog acting like King Kong; I admit that I laughed at her. No harm done: There were no subsequent incidents in my condo, beyond minor and appropriate incidents of sibling rivalry.

But Smartie's behavior in what should have been neutral territory was an entirely different matter. She charged people and other dogs in the street and on the sidewalk, usually waiting until they were passing us. It was evident from her demeanor that she'd perfected this act long before I got her.

I knew that if this behavior continued, she would one day provoke the wrong person or dog and end up hurt. And so I resisted the temptation to laugh it off. The next time she tried to charge someone, I gave her a quick, silent correction, which was instantly effective. But I remained on high alert for months afterward, poised to foil another surprise attack.

Whatever issue you're having with your small dog, the solution is really quite simple: Steel yourself to being bold enough to achieve the results you want. And stay ready to respond swiftly whenever the need arises.

Put Her on a Pedestal

One technique that I've found invaluable with any small dog is platform training. It's a great way to put a pooch on a pedestal without

Platform training comes in handy whenever I want to impress people and safeguard my dogs. Here, my Chihuahua mix, Able (left), and Chihuahua, Smartie, take a platform break during a performance at the Wisconsin State Fair.

turning her into a prima donna—in the process achieving an amazing level of behavioral and emotional control.

You don't need anything fancy—just a stable platform that's big enough to accommodate your dog comfortably and lightweight enough to move from room to room, toss in the car, and bring along on visits to friends and family members. It could be something as simple as a sturdy cardboard box turned upside down for a very small dog, or as fancy as a small table from an import store. I generally prefer something twenty to thirty-six inches high to make the difference between platform and off-limits areas very clear, although something much shorter can accomplish the same thing.

Training couldn't be simpler: Leash your dog and place her on the platform, holding her collar to keep her in place and praising her lavishly. Gradually slide your hand away from the collar, down the leash. If she attempts to jump off, grasp the collar once again. Continue working on this until she is staying reliably with a slack leash.

Then test her. Drop treats on the floor around her platform, petting and praising her if she stays, tightening the leash as necessary to keep her in place. Gradually increase the distractions, inviting friends to ring the doorbell and drop in. If she sits or lies down, that's fine; the only rule in platform training is that she mustn't leave her pedestal.

Once she's comfortable on her platform no matter what distractions you can rustle up at home, repeat the process in new areas. Some dogs might become reliable within an hour or two; others might require a couple of sessions.

Once your dog has mastered this skill, use it whenever you want an extra level of control—for instance, to keep her from begging at the table, jumping up on your guests, or chasing your host's cat, or when you want to protect her from other dogs or children without mollycoddling her. Simply put her on a table and don't let her jump off. You'll find that this training will also make your dog exceptionally well-behaved at the veterinarian and the groomer.

To platform-train your dog, first use her collar to steady her until she remains calmly in position. The only rule is that she mustn't leave her post.

Next, slide your hand down the leash, returning to the collar only if she tries to jump off the platform.

Get her accustomed to staying at her post even with a slack leash—and strengthen her resolve with increasingly tempting distractions.

A final note: Always use your hands to place and remove your dog from the pedestal. Teaching her to jump on and off is entirely possible, of course, but you'd need a much heavier, more stable platform, which means it wouldn't be portable. That would defeat one of the primary purposes of platform training: using this technique to maintain control when you're on the go.

Housetraining

Small hyper dogs are the most likely to soil in your home; in fact, this is probably the number-one problem I encounter with small dogs. It's important to note that a dog who resists housetraining or falls off the wagon may have a medical issue that needs attention. Bladder or kidney infections can derail the most determined dog's housetraining, spayed females may become incontinent, and certain medications can affect bladder and bowel habits. In most cases, the problem can be easily diagnosed and remedied, so check with your vet if you're having what seems to be an intractable house-soiling problem.

Even when health is not the issue, accidents are somewhat understandable with small hyper dogs: Even if they *know* they're supposed to go outside, they can have a tough time concentrating when they're there, because they are surrounded by all kinds of interesting sights, sounds, and smells. That means they may not relieve themselves adequately when they're given the opportunity. And when they're back inside, if anything excites or interests them, they may forget about holding it until the next trip outside.

If you want your hyper pooch to be reliably housetrained, help her along to rock-solid reliability with a combination of crating, supervision, stimulating chant, and high praise. That means crating her when you can't supervise. It means taking her outside immediately before and after crating and on a schedule tailored around her feeding routine and elimination tendencies—something you can determine only by observation and perhaps a little record-keeping.

It also means choosing an outdoor toileting area and, when she is about to relieve herself, repeating the mantra of your choice—"Potty hurry up" or "Sis boom bah," for instance—and then praising her when she does her business. Soon she'll go on command.

And it means that when she's out of her crate, she's in your sight wearing a collar with a leash attached. The moment you see her squatting or even sniffing around, leap into action: Jerk the leash, rush her out to your designated toileting area, repeat your chant, and praise her when she complies.

What it does *not* mean—ever—is punishing her after the fact, in any way. That can be both counterproductive and cruel.

Paper Training

Paper training is a reasonable alternative for small dogs—and it can be ideal for people who live in high-rise apartments or condos, as well as for owners whose ability to race outside has been compromised by age or disability. But understand that it's tough to have it both ways: If your ultimate goal is outdoor training, don't use paper training as an interim step; it will take that much more work to achieve your ultimate goal.

That said, here's how to paper train your small dog.

Start with a four-foot-square wire-mesh exercise pen—the sort you can find in pet supply stores and catalogs—and line it throughout with full-size newspapers at least five layers thick. For the first week, whenever you aren't watching her, keep your dog in the pen, changing the newspapers as often as necessary. Thereafter, begin reducing the size of the newspapered area. Devote a corner of the pen to a comfortable bed for the first week. Take away one piece of the newspaper the second week. Continue reducing the papered portion until you're left with just one full-size newspaper sheet.

Once your dog is using that newspaper reliably, you can leave the pen open to give her some freedom. But don't give her the run of the house quite yet; keep her confined in a fairly small room and increase her freedom only gradually when you can supervise her. If she attempts to eliminate elsewhere, pick her up and rush her back to the newspaper. Praise her for her success just as you would with outdoor training.

Whichever approach you use, understand that your dog will usually not be reliably housetrained for three to twelve months. So unless you're a gambler at heart, don't leave her alone on your new cream carpeting while you run errands. Still, after a few months of this intense duty, you should be able to let your guard down enough to lead a closer-to-normal life.

Medium Dogs

- Australian Shepherd
- Boxer
- Bulldog
- Cocker Spaniel
- Dalmatian
- Doberman Pinscher
- English Springer Spaniel
- German Shepherd Dog
- German Shorthaired Pointer

- Golden Retriever
- Labrador Retriever
- Pit Bull
- Rottweiler

When it comes to getting into mischief, there's nothing average about medium, hyper dogs. After all, they combine normal doggy curiosity with exquisitely developed senses and a most inconvenient height—a height that, given enough incentive, can put them in touch with all kinds of interesting things atop counters and tables, even when the laws of physics say these things should be out of their reach.

Genetics certainly play a role here. Many dogs of medium size have been bred with traits that are specifically optimized for their work. Sporting dogs, for instance, are bred for flushing, finding, and retrieving fowl in the field and from the water; scenthounds have been bred for trailing, rousing out, and treeing game; herding dogs, for gathering and moving stock; and working dogs, for patrolling, protection, and rescue. Take away the duties they've been genetically primed for and most will seek a replacement activity around the house.

There's no single or simple solution for the medium, hyper dog, except to provide adequate exercise, remove temptations whenever it's possible, and, whenever it's not, be ready to deliver a correction at the first sign of misbehavior.

That sign might be twitching nostrils when your dog notices that you've put out hors d'oeuvres for your guests, or playful circling of a neighbor who has wandered into her territory.

The correction might be silent delivery of a quick leash jerk. It might be a nose bop administered so stealthily that she doesn't even know what happened, except that it made her lose interest in whatever had caught her attention just moments before. Or it might be a curt "Leave it!" followed by effusive praise when she does just that.

Timing Is Everything

As it is in just about every other field of endeavor, timing your corrections is critical.

If you correct before the thought of misbehavior has formed in your dog's mind, it will only confuse her. What was *that* for? It might even make her think you're retracting a privilege you've already extended, such as joining you and your guests in the living room.

If you wait too long—until she has actually made contact with that leg of lamb or taken off with your nearly new reading glasses, for instance—you'll have a very tough time persuading her not to try it again next time she has a chance.

A young mother told me that she was having a recurring problem with her adolescent Lab stealing socks and toys out of her son's bedroom. She kept catching the dog hiding under the kitchen table, chewing on his loot. "I know he knows it's wrong," she reported, "because when I tell him to drop it, he always does." But his apparent guilt wasn't stopping him from committing the thefts in the first place.

It seemed to me that the only thing the dog's behavior proved was that he desperately wanted to please her—and I told her so. "After all, he instantly does what you tell him to do," I said. "He drops his loot on command. What you need to do is address the problem at its root, by catching him in the act of stealing and correcting him on the spot."

If you have a similar problem with your hyper dog, try entrapment: Snap a leash on her, let her follow you into the room, and busy yourself with the phone or computer, keeping one eye glued to her. If she approaches a sock or toy with a covetous look or twitching nostrils, quickly but unemotionally give the leash a snap.

If she stands by innocently, you need to up the ante. For instance, if socks are her usual prey, stuff one with a forbidden pleasure, such as a napkin you used when polishing off a platter of barbecued ribs. Then give her a little more space—standing just outside the door, for instance—to lower her perceived risk of being caught in the act. Eventually, she'll give in to her desires—and you can move in and make a quick correction to discourage future thefts.

Preproblem Training

You'll be way ahead of the game if you train your dog to respond properly *before* a potentially a disastrous situation arises. And the best way to do that is to set her up for the misbehaviors she finds most tempting.

Say, for instance, you worry most about her behavior when you serve snacks to company in the living room. Follow the entrapment procedure described above: Snap on a leash, put some people-food on the coffee table, and turn your back on her. If she eyes or sniffs at the treats, silently correct her. If she doesn't, observe her surreptitiously from a greater distance and repeat. Then try leaving the room without letting her out of your sight.

Don't discount the importance of teaching her other commands to prevent misbehavior or to stop a canine crime in progress. "Go to bed" can be invaluable when visual temptations seem to be winning the war. "Drop it" is priceless when she's already taken possession of forbidden goods.

Jumping

Medium, hyper dogs are generally more exuberant, friendly, and playful than their larger and smaller cousins. That means they're more likely to jump on people and other pets, often with surprising power and always to the victim's annoyance or fear. It also means they're the most likely to deliver a crotch assault or a well-timed body slam—running full force into another dog or the back of a human's legs—in the hope of inciting a riotous game of tag.

Fortunately, basic obedience training will usually build greater control, communication, and respect for your will—which may be enough to put an end to these problems. But if basic training doesn't quite do it and your problems persist, it's good to know there *are* simple solutions to most misbehavior.

For instance, jumping can be easily addressed with nose taps, standing on the leash, knee bumps, or foot slides. And even full-force body slamming can be controlled with basic obedience training and corrections, as long as the corrections are delivered swiftly, silently, and with finality.

The main prerequisite is being prepared by snapping a leash on your dog before the next victim arrives.

Large Dogs

- American Bulldog
- Bernese Mountain Dog
- Bloodhound
- Bull Mastiff
- Great Dane
- Irish Wolfhound
- Newfoundland
- Scottish Deerhound
- Greyhound
- St. Bernard

Large dogs don't have to be very hyper before their behavior becomes troublesome. It's size itself that creates the problem, even more than attitude.

Teaching Your Dog to Back Up

Unnecessary and largely useless in smaller breeds, the "back" command is invaluable for large dogs. Here's how to teach it.

Stand in front of your leashed dog in a narrow passageway—between two cars in a garage, for instance, or between a couch and a large coffee table. Shorten the leash and move your hand close to the collar. Tell her "back" and give the leash a little backwards jerk as you shuffle into her rather quickly. When she takes a step backward, praise her cheerfully.

This isn't a natural movement for most dogs, so you might want to take it a step at a time. Once she's mastered one step back, increase it to two and then three, then more.

You'll be surprised at how often this command comes in handy!

A Bull in a China Shop

That's exactly what a large dog is like, especially in a house that's smaller than a mansion. She'll get herself into places from which she won't be able to extract herself without knocking over everything. She'll clear entire end tables of trinkets simply by standing nearby and wagging her tail. She'll take what she thinks is a gentle approach to greeting the little old lady next door and wind up breaking the poor woman's hip.

There's rarely any malicious intent. In fact, large dogs tend to be extraordinarily sweet and loving. Many like to sit on laps and lean up against humans of all sizes. And some adore exploring the tactile side of their personalities; they want to reach out and touch a beloved human, sometimes pawing insistently at their victims.

All very endearing, and, fortunately, very controllable using techniques that your big buddy will find great fun, such as Play during Training—a useful technique with many applications for dogs of all sizes.

If you're the proud owner of a big dog, you'll also want to teach her the "back" command (see the box on this page).

Just Plain Powerful

The trouble with a large dog is that she is usually powerful beyond her wildest dreams—and, pound for pound, a lot stronger than most handlers could ever hope to be. The trick to controlling all that brute strength is to harness the mechanical advantages of leverage—and to remain aware of both your dog and your surroundings, so that you'll be able to act promptly to capitalize on these advantages.

For instance, if you perform a Sneakaway (explained in chapter 3) while there's still some slack in the leash, you can effectively triple or quadruple your body weight; the more slack and speed, the better your leverage. If you wait until she's got the momentum and is pulling you down the street, on the other hand, you may have to settle for trying to steer her until she runs out of steam.

Special Tools

The main problem with super-size hyper dogs is that they may not even be aware that you're around when they're pursuing their own agendas. You may be out for a nice little walk in the park with your St. Bernard, for instance, when she takes off after a bunny, dragging you in her wake. Even if you pull on the leash with all your might, she probably won't even notice. For this reason, it's very important to train a large dog in increasingly distracting environments, and to always be mentally prepared to monopolize every last ounce of leverage that's available.

It's also why you will want to consider making a minor investment in equipment that can make a major difference in your dog's responsiveness—and could one day save her life. I'm talking about more than a well-fitting collar and wide, nonslip leash in leather or Biothane—both minimum-standard training tools. I'm talking about devices such as:

- No-jump or no-pull harness
- Head halter
- Slip collar
- Prong collar
- Belly band

These tools are perfect for anyone who is in danger of losing the battle of strength with a large dog. If that describes you, experiment until you find the tool that's right for your dog; you will not regret it.

MOLDING CHARACTER

More important than the size of your dog is her character—or, to be more precise, her reactions or responses to you as her trainer and handler.

Character is usually more important than any innate quality you can think of. While intelligence can sometimes be helpful, for example, teachability is the trait that makes a dog a joy to work with. While picking concepts up quickly is nice, what serves us best in the long run is an eagerness to learn—along with our own perseverance and delight in working with this curious creature who has so much to teach us.

Astute owners appreciate resilience over spunk, cooperation over independence. And we do our best to develop such qualities in our dogs, while discouraging every last trace of poutiness, manipulation, and resentment. The fact is, a dog's character evolves over time. And we can do a great deal to facilitate her progress.

Let's take a look at a few examples of dogs with undesirable character traits, and the best way to begin shaping them into the well-behaved creatures we all love.

Defensive Duke

Is your dog generally well-behaved on the leash and around the house—but bitterly resentful of corrections? Does he bristle at your attempts to control or direct him, perhaps even marking the house or growling at you? These are signs of defensiveness, which requires careful handling. It can appear in dogs of any size or breed, but is more common in males of larger working breeds.

The basic rule with such dogs is to spend extra time teaching, to minimize the frequency of corrections. Always remain calm, firmly guiding your dog to make the right choices. Avoid eye contact and emotion, but offer him brief but frequent and enthusiastic verbal praise when he's earned it. Whenever his attention wanders, recapture it with a Sneakaway before resuming a command. In fact, Sneakaways will probably be your best friend in working with such a dog. They enable you to capture his attention without trying to boss him around, which doesn't work with Defensive Duke; after a few Sneakaways, he'll start naturally looking to you as his boss.

Sensitive Sally

Instead of the normal exuberance we expect from hyper dogs, some are sensitive, timid, and withdrawn. When we finally stop coddling them and try to train them, they collapse; they become instant drama queens whose goal in life is convincing us that they're incapable of doing what we ask.

If this sounds like your dog, ignore such tantrums at all costs. Instead, proceed with each training session, keeping your pace and tone lively and cheerful and your corrections and praise short and perky. Avoid eye contact, touching, and verbal corrections, and ignore your dog's hysterics. Remember, if you give her a job to do and then make it as easy as possible for her to do it, she won't have time to be obsessed with herself.

Dizzy Dora

Some overly exuberant dogs act like they're putting most of their energy into directionless hyperdrive and not a shred into forming a complete thought. That's probably not at all the case, but, like flighty people, such critters mask their intelligence with a flurry of nonstop activity.

If this is your dog, you'll have to work to keep her attention. Monotone delivery and uninspired corrections won't help this dog focus. Instead, move quickly through your training routine, varying the order to keep her attention on you, adding new challenges to make her think, and praising her as if she'd just won the Nobel Prize.

Don't Give Up

Just about any dog is capable of learning the basics of obedience training. But every dog has certain aptitudes that will make her better at specific commands. For instance, an independent dog like a Rhodesian Ridgeback will probably have an easier time with the "stay" than will a Cavalier King Charles Spaniel. But the Cavalier might be more of a natural at coming when called or heeling than the Ridgeback.

Regardless of aptitude, every dog is capable of learning to do all of these things. You may simply have to increase your repetitions when the task runs counter to your dog's character.

Interestingly, I've found that over time, the mistake-prone dog often becomes more reliable at a given command. Working through her mistakes can actually crystallize her understanding of once-troublesome tasks. Which means it's best to just stay on your game plan, adjusting the rate of your progress to fit your dog's capabilities. Don't become impatient or emotional if she has a tough time picking up a particular command.

Miraculous Changes?

With the right training, some of your dog's character traits will change over the course of your lives together.

My first dog, a Siberian Husky named Tess, weighed just forty-five pounds, but I was a little kid and she'd been bred to pull sleds. When she got excited—which happened whenever a new person came near, especially if that person said a word directly to her—she would totally wig out in her joy. I spent our early months together taking her to the local dog training club and holding my breath, hoping no one would approach us.

And then we discovered the sit-stay.

It was the turning point in our lives together. Tess was really good at the sit-stay. And through it she discovered how to control herself emotionally. Even though she remained sociable her entire life, once she'd mastered this simple command, she maintained a level of dignity even when she wasn't in a sit-stay.

Kiwi and Weaselle—a Japanese Chin and a Briard—were initially very slow learners for me. During our early obedience training, they both seemed somewhat perplexed by the "finish," a maneuver requiring the dog to return to the heel position after responding to a recall. While most dogs can pick up this simple maneuver in a week or two, Kiwi and Weas were still struggling months into our training sessions.

But eventually they caught on. And suddenly, everything became relatively easy for them. Kiwi went on to become an AKC Obedience Trial Champion, and Weas earned his Utility Dog obedience title before he turned 3.

Maybe it was our arduous work together that did it, by solidifying our bonds and our persistence. Or maybe it was just some mental roadblock in these dogs that, once removed, left the way clear for unimpeded learning.

Despite the fact that she learned relatively slowly, Japanese Chin Ch. and OTCh Kiwi will always be one of my all-time favorite dogs because she had so much heart. This photo was taken in 1989.

And don't excuse your dog from learning by projecting human emotions on her. She's probably not balking at this command because she's confused or scared or feeling abused. She's most likely just learning by thinking it all through—a process that mimics human learning patterns.

The amazing thing is that with most dogs, mastering just one simple command can often flip the switch that controls character, turning them into new creatures overnight (see the box on page 27).

The moral of the story? Hang in there, no matter how long it seems to be taking.

MANAGING TEMPERAMENT

Is your hyper dog basically aggressive or retiring? Shy or outgoing? Temperamental or stable? Nervous or confident? These traits are all the result of basic canine temperament, which is the product of heredity, neurology, or environment—or a combination of these.

Even the most experienced professional can only speculate on which variables have contributed to an individual dog's temperament. And the causes are generally irrelevant to proper training and management—which is precisely what is needed to prevent a temperament-challenged dog from feeling threatened or posing a threat to others.

The first step is determining if your dog has any temperament issues. To find out, take a look at the quiz on pages 30 and 31.

IMPROVING WITH AGE

Age can be another huge factor in managing a hyper dog—one that must be accounted for and respected.

Puppyhood

It's often said that popular breeds such as Labrador and Golden Retrievers are uncontrollable or unteachable the first two years, but thereafter turn into the best possible dogs. But that's not necessarily so, and the changes are not automatic. Puppyhood is indeed temporary. But a puppy's naughtiness, if left uncorrected, can last a lifetime.

Never assume you can ignore poor behavior for the first couple of years and still have everything work out fine in the end. If you ignore it, your dog is likely to need expert intervention or a new home.

Old Age

The aging hyper dog presents an entirely different set of problems. There are times when you'll want to be patient and times when you'll be justified in taking action.

I have seen a wide range of senile behaviors over the years—everything from pacing, panting, and barking jags to climbing on once-forbidden furniture and destroying various household items. If any such behaviors arise in your aging dog, your first stop should be a visit to your veterinarian. In fact, let your vet know about *any* behavioral changes in an aging dog to find out if there are organic causes that can be treated or assuaged—perhaps via a special vet-recommended diet or medication, or using the feng shui techniques described in chapter 6.

But in many cases, aging hyper dogs simply need more exercise combined with mental stimulation. Try an obedience refresher course using the techniques described in this book; it will probably do wonders for your senior.

Obedience training may also do the trick if you've inherited or adopted an older dog who is exhibiting undesirable hyper behaviors. You *can* teach an old dog new tricks!

Not long ago, a woman brought a 12-year-old Husky into one of our two-session Manners classes. The dog began raising a ruckus the minute he walked into the studio—barking, snarling, straining at the leash, and lunging at the closest classmates.

I invited them outside and within a minute had quieted him down, using Bitter Apple corrections. The woman then told me that she'd recently married the Husky's lifelong owner. The dog had never had any training or socialization with other canines, she said, and his behavior was intolerable.

The dog had a number of good qualities, as it turned out: Despite his advancing years, he was remarkably vigorous and healthy. And the new wife was open-minded, willing, and receptive to new ideas, and refused to make excuses for the dog's behavior. She was also very watchful—an important quality, because it meant she was mentally prepared to take action quickly.

Over the course of the next week, she diligently applied the techniques we discussed that night. And the following week, she came to class with what looked like a new dog: He was relaxed, controlled, and ready to learn. He still had a ways to go, but I'm confident that she is making his last years just as happy as they can be, as he develops confidence and enjoys the mental stimulation associated with solid obedience training.

What's Your Dog's Temperament?

Perhaps your hyper dog is well-socialized and well-trained but still reacts adversely in certain situations. This may indicate a temperament problem, or it may indicate that she isn't as well trained as you think she is. This quiz should help you evaluate the nuances of your dog's temperament—and, in the long run, help you gain control over anything troublesome you discover.

As you go through it, keep a few things in mind:

- Even consistently "stable" responses may warrant special handling in certain circumstances, to guard against any of these behaviors escalating into potentially dangerous acts.
- It's not uncommon for a dog to be adorable in all situations except one—being aggressive with food or toys, for instance, or insecure around strangers.
- Most dogs will eventually display the entire temperament spectrum to some degree, depending on the situation. For instance, even very timid dogs can sometimes become domineering, and ordinarily domineering dogs can occasionally shrink into a corner.
- As her director, your goal is to respond appropriately to the behavior your dog is displaying at the moment—not to her "normal" behavior.

The sentences in parentheses below will give you an indication of the probable cause of each reaction—and a head start on addressing any problems related to temperament. It's definitely a thinking person's game!

1. Sensitivity to noise
When there is a thunderstorm or fireworks, my dog:

- a. Jumps in the bathtub, drools, and shakes. (He's noise-sensitive, but if this behavior is strictly situational, it may not be a problem.)
- b. Sits by the door waiting to run out and jump into a puddle. (A stable response—your dog must be a retriever!)

2. Emotional sensitivity
When I watch football games on television, I yell a lot. My dog:

- a. Runs for cover. (It's time to give your dog a break and quiet down.)
- b. Waits for me to dump the popcorn bowl. (This is a stable reaction and also demonstrates that your dog is an opportunist.)

3. Sociability with people
When company arrives, my dog:

- a. Is closeted in another room because I fear for my guests' safety. (She is antisocial.)
- b. Jumps on them and licks them all over if I give her the chance. (She's a stable dog.)
- c. Is suspicious and leery and growls if they attempt to make friends with her. (She is potentially insecure, potentially aggressive.)
- d. Is suspicious and leery and runs away if they try to make friends with her. (She is insecure and lacks confidence.)
- e. Seems just fine at first but can turn on a dime, for no apparent reason. (She's definitely aggressive—unpredictably so.)

4. Sociability with other dogs
When I take my dog for a walk and we encounter another canine, my dog:

   a. Always goes nuts, pulling, barking, growling, staring, or lunging at her foe. (She is aggressive—perhaps dangerously so.)
   b. Is fine unless the other dog is excited or has certain physical characteristics that seem to set her off. (More aggressive behavior. Just as in the first scenario, it's time to seriously work on control around distractions.)
   c. She wants to investigate and play or acknowledges them and just keeps ambling along. (Good, stable dog!)
   d. Wants to run away. (She's timid and lacks confidence.)

5. Sociability with children
Around kids, my dog:

   a. Is aware of them but shows no sign of uneasiness. (She is one sound canine.)
   b. Tries to escape, her eyes big with fear. (Her confidence has deserted her.)
   c. Barks and lunges at them. (She's aggressive and must be controlled.)
   d. Wants to jump, play, and lick schmutz off their faces. (She represents the epitome of stable dogdom.)
   e. Seems fine but may jump or snap at them without warning. (This is potentially dangerous instability.)

6. Possessiveness
When my dog is around her toys or food and I approach, she:

   a. Willingly relinquishes them to me. (She's of sound temperament in this situation.)
   b. Tenses up and uses her body to cover her most highly prized possessions. (She is territorial.)
   c. May charge at me. (She's aggressive and unstable.)

7. Reaction to strangers
When my dog encounters a stranger:

   a. She holds her ground, tenses up, and rejects the stranger's kindness. (She's unstable and potentially aggressive.)
   b. The harder the person tries to befriend her, the more suspicious she becomes. (She exhibits unstable tendencies.)
   c. She accepts the person unquestioningly, just as she does my family and friends. (She is a stable pooch.)

8. Road trips
When my dog is in the car, she:

   a. Barks with interest at the passing scene. (That's stable but obnoxious and begs for reform.)
   b. Charges if someone approaches the car. (This could demonstrate aggressiveness and territoriality.)
   c. Bites at the windows during travel. (This, too, could indicate aggressiveness.)

9. Reaction to the environment
When encountering certain inanimate objects—street grates, open staircases, garbage cans, etc.—my dog:

   a. Is unfazed. (She is stable.)
   b. Hesitates, looks at the object, and continues on her way. (She's cautious, but stable.)
   c. Barks and backs away with her hackles raised. (She lacks confidence.)
   d. Stops dead in her tracks and will not proceed. (No confidence here at all.)

Chapter 3

Achieving Control

Communication and training essentials

....

"**I** just want him to calm down. He's way too hyper for me!"

This is a complaint I hear regularly. But the problem is usually not that the dog has a hyperactive nature or a super-abundance of excess energy; it's much more likely that he is just not listening or understanding. Bring his listening skills up to an acceptable standard and *voila*! Hyperactivity will no longer be a problem.

Communication is the very simple secret of transforming a hyper dog into the ultimate companion. It is also the foundation of all obedience training. When you start training your dog, you are essentially developing a vocabulary for helping him understand exactly what it is you want him to do. With this understanding, the bond between you and your hyper dog can begin to grow. Before long, you'll be in sync with one another. And then suddenly (and perhaps surprisingly), you'll begin to see problematic behaviors diminishing or disappearing entirely.

The best news is that none of this is rocket science. Just about any dog can learn these basics and blossom into a great companion, as long as you are willing to put some time into it.

That's not to say that plain old exercise is unimportant. It is *very* important for every dog, and without it, the hyper dog's bad manners will become even more horrid. In fact, we'll look at some ways to quickly burn off excess energy in the next chapter. But exercise alone won't transform a hyper dog into a nearly perfect companion. Only the mental stimulation and communication of obedience training can do that.

So give it a try. I promise that it will be well worth the effort!

A hyper dog who spends his walks pulling, weaving, and jumping around may need more exercise—but that's the least of his problems.

A FEW CASES THAT PROVE THE POINT

"A casual walk around the neighborhood does nothing to relieve my dog's hyperness," Amiable Dog Training assistant Tom Pender says of his Rottweiler, Harley. "He needs the stimulation that training provides to calm down." Making his hyper dog *think* is absolutely critical to controlling those ever-present hyper tendencies, Tom says.

"Without that mental challenge, exercise leaves my dog excited and restless. If I walk with him leading the way, on a loose leash instead of heeling, I'm not providing him with all that he needs."

Rose Pickering, a former Amiable student, volunteers at the Wisconsin Humane Society in addition to training her own canine crew. She has ample opportunity to work with dogs who could best be described as out of control. But it doesn't faze her. "Dogs have been selectively bred for centuries to help humans with their work," Rose points out, "and they are never happier than when they are working to please you. A neglected dog will jump to get our attention, but if he is redirected from an undesirable behavior to a desirable one—a 'sit,' for instance—he gets our attention as well as our approval. He's working for us, bonding with us, and that makes him happy."

Even the most hyper dogs thrive on the intellectual exercise associated with obedience training. It turns walks into a true pleasure for dog and owner alike.

Tom and Natalie Pender say the mental stimulation of obedience train-ing has transformed their hyper Rottweiler, Harley, into an outstanding companion.

Over the years, many of my students have reported that obedience training has made an enormous difference in their relationships with their hyper dogs. "I feel most bonded to my dog when we're training," one told me recently. "At least one night a week, that's how we get our exercise. The bond felt there is a pretty natural side effect. And when she's responding well in training, she seems much happier and calmer."

Sometimes obedience training can even change the balance of affec-tion in a multidog household. Not long ago, a couple with a beloved 4-year-old Cocker Spaniel decided to get a second dog, an adult, from Cocker Spaniel Rescue. The problems started immediately. The new dog growled at anyone who approached his possessions. And the more com-fortable he became in the household, the nastier he became.

The wife took him to an obedience class, to no avail. In despera-tion, she called me in for private, on-site training. Much to her surprise, underneath the dog's crankiness we discovered a spirit of cooperation. So remarkable was the transformation that the new Cocker has taken some of the shine off their beloved older pooch, who now seems spoiled in comparison.

"Every dog needs a job," says Rose Pickering, shown here with her well-employed Norwich Terrier, Dolly, husband, James, and Dandie Dinmont Terrier, Lloyd.

This is not at all unusual. And the remedy is easy: Train them both!

THE BASICS

The basic obedience training discussed in this chapter will affect your dog's behavior, both directly and indirectly. Applied consistently and regularly, it should transform him into the canine companion you've always longed for.

Before you begin, set aside all your preconceptions about your dog's natural abilities and character. You really can't know how trainable he is until you've given him a fair shot. That means first developing your skills and then developing his by practicing together 15 minutes a day, every day for four weeks. Feel free to break the sessions up into several shorter lessons each day, if it's more convenient.

Here's what you'll need to get started:

- A collar he can't back out of—a slip, prong, or snug buckle-type collar.
- A six-foot leather, Beta, or Biothane leash (see some examples at www.tackatack.com); the larger the dog, the wider the leash should be.

Establish a Code of Conduct

To get the best possible return on your training investment, commit yourself to these simple rules.

Be consistent.
Whether you're at home, at the groomer's or vet's, or in the training field, abide by the same rules of behavior.

Say what you mean and mean what you say.
Teach and enforce simple commands, such as "sit," "down," "stay," and "come," as you go about your daily business. This builds in your dog a work ethic, concentration in spite of distractions, and an understanding that you're always ready, willing, and able to follow through.

Don't yell.
Don't threaten, repeat yourself, chase fruitlessly, or grab at the dog, either. If that's all you do, and you never follow through, your hyper dog will simply tune you out, oblivious to your ranting, whenever anything more amusing is going on.

Instead, correct or redirect.
Be ready to do one or the other whenever your dog misbehaves.

Mix pleasure with business.
Make learning fun by punctuating even the most serious obedience sessions with frequent bursts of rollicking games—running, hiding, pounding, playful nudging, retrieving, and teasing your dog with his favorite toys.

Keep a line on your dog.
Untrained and undertrained dogs of all ages should be kept on a leash whenever they're not confined—and that's especially true of hyper dogs. It's the only way to stop them from unleashing all manner of misbehavior and destruction, to redirect their energy into playing with toys or learning and obeying commands, and to keep them safely at your side.

Don't smother your dog.
Rejoice when your dog flirts with other people. In fact, ask experienced friends to take him for walks. This builds confidence and keeps him from becoming overly dependent on you.

- A fifteen-foot-longe line, a special type of leash that you'll use for many of the procedures described in this book. (Not many pet supply stores carry longe lines, but you can make your own easily and inexpensively. Head over to a hardware store and buy fifteen feet of nylon cord—a quarter-inch in diameter for a medium dog, an eighth-inch for a small dog, and three-eighths of an inch for a large one. Buy a swivel snap, too, and tie it on one end of the line. On the other end, make a loop for your thumb. That's all there is to it!)

If you choose a slip collar for training, position the dog on your left and the ring you clip the leash to so that the chain tightens toward the dog's back.

- A fifty-foot light line that you can tie on to your dog's collar; Venetian-blind cord, available from most hardware stores, is ideal.

- Gloves to protect your hands from burns when using the light line.

- A bottle of Bitter Apple chewing deterrent, used to fill up a small spray bottle that you can hide in the palm of your hand.

- A shaker can, made by dropping eight pennies in an empty soda can and taping the top closed.

This is the wrong way to put on a slip collar. The chain tightens toward the dog's front and will not release quickly.

The techniques described here are best suited to dogs 16 weeks and older. For puppies between 8 and 15 weeks old, skip this section and concentrate, instead, on developing a foundation of good manners (page 93).

A fifteen-foot longe line is a must. (See page 39 or visit www.dogclass.com for details.)

You'll also need a fifty-foot light line to tie on your dog's collar. Venetian-blind cord from a hardware store is perfect.

The Sneakaway

If I had to pick a Most Valuable Training Technique for the hyper dog, it would probably be the Sneakaway. The fact is, learning cannot begin unless your dog's attention is focused on you. And the Sneakaway is the best way I know of to get and keep a dog's attention, while improving his responsiveness to all your training efforts.

The principle is simple: When your dog goes north without your approval, you go south. When he heads west, you head east.

There are three phases to mastering the Sneakaway.

Phase One

To get started, head for a large area that has no obstructions—fifty feet square or larger is ideal—and snap a longe line on your dog's collar. Then:

1. Slip the thumb of one hand through the handle and wrap your fingers around the handle to make your grip as secure as possible without compromising your ability to release it in a split second. Then plant both hands on your midsection to prevent you from inadvertently jerking your dog.

2. Stroll around.

3. The moment your dog becomes distracted and is not paying attention to you, turn and walk briskly in the opposite direction. If he doesn't follow immediately, the line will tighten abruptly.

4. Watch where you're going; don't watch your dog. You'll know when his attention is back on you and you alone.

If the line gets wrapped in his legs, resist the urge to untangle it. You want him to learn by experience how to navigate around the line. After a session or two, he'll be able to keep his legs tangle-free and his focus 100 percent on you.

If he heads east, you head west.

The line will tighten abruptly, recapturing your dog's attention and putting him in hot pursuit of you.

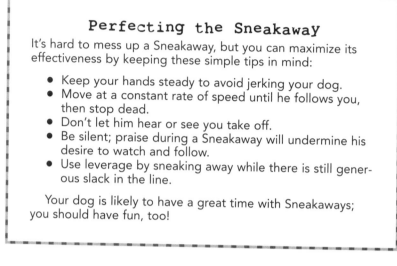

Perfecting the Sneakaway

It's hard to mess up a Sneakaway, but you can maximize its effectiveness by keeping these simple tips in mind:

- Keep your hands steady to avoid jerking your dog.
- Move at a constant rate of speed until he follows you, then stop dead.
- Don't let him hear or see you take off.
- Be silent; praise during a Sneakaway will undermine his desire to watch and follow.
- Use leverage by sneaking away while there is still generous slack in the line.

Your dog is likely to have a great time with Sneakaways; you should have fun, too!

Phase Two

When your dog is watching you and keeping his legs tangle-free, begin introducing the kinds of distractions that are most tempting to your dog (see the box on page 44).

As soon as he's distracted, don't just walk in the opposite direction; run! When he begins following you, stop dead in your tracks. As long as he's paying attention to you, stand still or amble around. The moment he turns his attention elsewhere, do the Sneakaway again.

Training with distractions helps your dog focus exclusively on you. Other dogs, a person, and a toy are heavy distractions; work up to them gradually.

For leashed Sneakaways, here's how to position your hands and the leash. First, put your thumb through the loop . . .

. . . then close your fingers over the handle . . .

Continue practicing this technique, introducing more tempting distractions and running faster during your Sneakaways. Within a relatively short time, this exercise will teach him to pay attention to you in just about any circumstances.

Phase Three

Once your dog is content to hang on your every move in anticipation of a Sneakaway, substitute your six-foot leash for the longe line. Put your right thumb in the handle and wrap your fingers around the loop. Gather up the slack in that hand too, leaving just enough so that the leash is not quite taut when your right hand is at your right hip (or, if your dog is very tall or very short, at your navel). Your left hand will remain free.

. . . and finally, take up the slack in the same hand and position your hand against your body somewhere between your navel and outer thigh, wherever it's comfortable.

Lifesaving Distractions

When your dog is responding to your commands instantly, begin introducing a series of escalating distractions into your daily routine. This will teach him to pay attention to you even in situations in which other hyper dogs would have a meltdown.

Use your imagination to create tempting distractions. Here are some idea-starters:

- Place toys or treats around the training area. (Soup bones can be almost irresistible.)
- Surreptitiously toss treats around so that they seem to be appearing out of nowhere.
- Ask a friend to ring the doorbell, enter your home, and make himself comfortable.
- Take the dog to places with lots of adults, children, and dogs.

Distraction-assisted training always begins with Sneakaways. But once you've exhausted your ability to distract your dog during this phase of training, you'll also use this technique to ensure rock-solid obedience to each command you teach him.

When you begin applying distractions to such commands as "sit," "down," and "stay," insist that your dog obey until you release him with a "chin-touch okay." When he responds to the distraction rather than to you, quickly correct him. If your dog becomes so distracted that enforcing commands has become impossible, help him regain his composure with Sneakaways punctuated by colossal distractions.

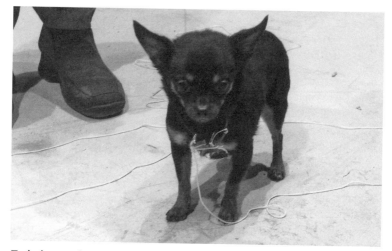

To help my dog Smartie understand that my command takes precedence over her favorite distraction, I "dress" her with the appropriate equipment—in this case, the light line.

Remember, the goal is to keep your dog focused on you and obedient to you, no matter what is going on around you—especially in emergencies. This simple teaching tool could one day save your dog's life.

I then let her indulge in the distraction; she's a sucker for fresh meat.

Finally, I enforce the "come" and keep my hands close to my body, bending down to her level so that she doesn't dance around just out of my reach.

Stroll around again, as usual. The moment your dog gets distracted by something or someone, drop the slack, pivot to the right, and run away. When he follows you, stop dead and pick up the slack again.

Your dog will most likely enjoy Sneakaways immensely; after all, running with you is fun and exciting! He'll quickly learn to pay attention to you in the hope that you'll be able to run together again. And he'll learn that he can avoid the correction of the tightened leash by "catching you" before it tightens up.

"Sit"

There are many ways to teach basic commands such as "sit." Here's the approach I've found to be the simplest and most reliable.

1. Hold your dog's collar with one hand and place the other hand on his loin—that is, across his back, along his waistline.

2. Command "sit" while pulling up and slightly forward on his collar and lightly pushing down on his rear.

3. Praise him as sits.

4. Once he's in place, release him with the "chin-touch okay"—a gentle forward stroke under the jaw accompanied by a cheerful "okay."

Super "Sits," "Stays," and "Comes"

For the best results teaching your dog just about any command, keep these tips in mind:

- To ensure reliable obedience, work around distractions even in the beginning stages of training.
- Never repeat commands, and issue them only when you can enforce them.
- Praise your dog both during and after the fact.
- Following this praise, release your dog from the command with the "chin-touch okay"—that is, inviting him to move forward by gently touching under his jaw while cheerfully saying "okay."
- If he's resistant or inattentive, be especially firm when positioning him and extra quick to release him.
- If he becomes difficult, practice some Sneakaways.

Use the "chin-touch okay" to release your dog from a position. As you say "okay!" in a bright tone of voice, give his throat a gentle forward stroke. This invites him to move forward on his own.

Once he knows this command, if he refuses to sit out of laziness or because he's distracted, correct him by simultaneously giving a quick upward jerk on the leash and a light-handed but steady downward push on his rear. After a few weeks, you'll be able to correct a refusal to sit simply by jerking upward on the leash.

"Down"

The "down" position induces a state of relative calm in any dog. That makes it an essential command for the hyper dog to master. In a proper "down," your dog can't leap or roll around or even crawl forward until you've released him. And he won't want to: Within moments, he should be relaxed enough to maintain this position—eventually, even when strong distractions are vying for his attention.

To put your dog in the down position with a single word, practice this procedure:

1. Place your left thumb and index finger along opposite sides of your dog's spine just behind his shoulder blades.

2. Take his collar in your right hand.

3. As you command "down," use a pressure-point push to gently push him downward with your left hand while pulling him down with your right hand.

4. Once he's down, praise him by petting his tummy, and then release him with the "chin-touch okay."

5. Practice this for a week or until he eagerly responds to your push. Then, to improve the speed of his response or enforce the "down" command if he dallies, change your approach slightly: Snap on a leash and give him a few moments to respond to "down." If he doesn't, use your left hand to apply a pressure-point push as usual and jerk down on the leash with your right.

To enforce the "down" command or improve his speed, use a pressure-point push with your left hand . . .

. . . while jerking the leash down with your right hand.

After about fifty repetitions, your dog should melt into the down position. Now you can begin weaning him from the hand contact.

Placing him on your left side, proceed as above, but this time grip the leash just below the snap instead of holding the collar. Then, as you command "down," place both hands on the leash and jerk it back toward the dog's right hind foot.

After a few dozen repetitions of this technique, your dog should respond to the "down" command without any physical reminder. If he doesn't, quickly correct him using the technique I've just described.

"Come"

Hyper dogs are notoriously impulsive. If yours got away, could you stop him from charging through an open door, across a street, or through a park?

Don't reach out for a hyper dog who is responding to "come." Instead, keep your arms to yourself so he'll learn that "come" means getting close enough to snuggle.

No? That's why "come" is probably the most important command you will ever teach your hyper dog. You'll want to make sure you spend an adequate amount of time working on it. Here's how to do it:

1. Leash your dog and wait for him to be distracted.
2. Call him by name, adding the "come" command (for example, "Seymour, come!") and use the leash to reel him in as you back away, saying "good, good, goooooood!" If necessary, give the leash a quick jerk.
3. Squat down to celebrate his arrival, but don't block his approach by reaching out to pet him; that will only teach him that "come" means approaching you and then having a rousing game of keep-away.
4. Release him with the "chin-touch okay."

Because this approach enables you to keep your hands to yourself, engages your dog with verbal praise, and encourages him to remain close to you until he's released, he'll quickly begin to cozy up to you when he hears you say "come."

After you've practiced for a week, stop reeling in the leash. Instead, just call the dog and wait a second to see if he responds. If he does, back up and praise him as usual. If he ignores you, jerk the leash toward you as you back up and praise him.

"Heel"

Although certain dogs require extensive practice, heeling is a really valuable skill to teach. Instead of the more common and less clear leash-jerking approach, I recommend a go-opposite technique that's all in your legs. Following the Sneakaway philosophy, accelerate—either straight forward or following a change of direction—whenever your dog tries to leave the heel position.

Here's the procedure:

1. Position your dog on your left side, holding the leash in your right hand with your thumb through the loop and the slack in your palm.
2. Command, "Seymour, heel" and walk forward briskly.
3. Before slowing to a stop, smoothly move your right hand down the leash close to your dog's collar.

With the dog on your left side, hold the leash in your right hand with your thumb through the loop. Gather the slack in your palm and position that hand on your right hip or navel or somewhere in between; don't hold it any higher, and keep it next to your body.

Second, using your dog's name, command "heel" and move ahead briskly.

Third, before stopping, slide your right hand down the leash to the collar.

Finally, as you stop, make him sit by pulling up on the collar with your right hand and pushing down on his rear with your left.

4. As you stop, make him sit by pulling upward on the collar while using your left hand to push downward on his rear.

5. Praise him as he responds.

Although this will all eventually become automatic (including the "sit"), he's going to be a little sloppy at first. As long as he's paying attention to you and walking at your left side in spite of distractions, that's great.

Eventually, the "sit" will become automatic and your hyper dog will be a pleasure to walk.

Ideally, your dog will walk alongside you in the heel position without letting anything distract him.

If he becomes distracted or starts forging ahead, drop the slack in the leash and do a Sneakaway 180 degrees to your right. When he pursues you, return to your normal pace and leash grip.

If he becomes distracted or starts forging ahead, simply drop the slack in the leash and do a Sneakaway 180 degrees to the right. When he tries to catch up, return to your normal pace and leash grip.

Once he has this casual form of heeling down, you can teach him a more precise heeling position by using 90-degree turns.

If he is forging ahead but is still within a few inches of the proper position, do the Jackie Gleason "Away We Go" left turn: Grasp the leash with your left hand to create slight upward tension on the collar. Then turn left, walking into your dog's path with your left leg first. Your "klutziness" will persuade him to watch you more intently and maintain a better position in the future. (If your dog is small, keep your

If he's forging but is within inches of the proper heel position, do the Jackie Gleason "Away We Go" left turn. Grab the slack with your left hand and turn left into his path.

feet close to the ground as you walk into his path; the point is to shuffle into him, not trample or kick him.)

If he is lagging, heeling wide, sniffing the ground, or seems inattentive, do the Mikhail Baryshnikov right turn: Step in a new direction with your right foot and leap an imaginary five-foot broad jump with your left foot first. Keep your left hand off the leash; you want the leash to be bumped forward by your thigh as you leap. For small dogs, take your broad jump down a few notches; you want to leap forward, but only by two or three feet.

Before long, these techniques should teach your dog to stay in the heel position even on a slack leash.

To teach the automatic "sit" during heeling, use the procedure I've just described for several days, helping him sit with both the upward pull on the collar and the downward push on the rear. After a few days, start eliminating the downward push and substitute an upward jerk for

If he lags, heels too far from you, or seems inattentive, take a Mikhail Baryshnikov right turn. Step in a new direction with your right foot and then leap an imaginary five-foot broad jump with your left leg to bump the leash forward.

the pull as you take your last step before stopping.

Within a few more days, try eliminating the jerk to see if your dog will sit without this cue when you stop. If not, keep using the jerk for a few days until the "sit" becomes automatic.

Always greet his obedience with praise, even if you had to use a reminder.

To cure sloppy "sits," for instance, if he swings his rear away from you in order to face you, heel forward and try again, jerking up on the leash as you take your final step before stopping completely. If he sits out of position again, go back to using the jerk *and* push, helping him into a fast, straight "sit" on your next five halts.

Never attempt to reposition a sloppy "sit" with your hands alone. Instead, monitor his position as you halt and use the leash, your movement, and your hands as described.

"Sit-Stay"

This is another critical skill any dog should master—and it's mandatory for the hyper dog. "Sit-stay" is a four-part process.

Phase One

1. Position your dog in a sit. He will expect to be released with a "chin-touch okay."

2. Instead, hold the leash taut over his head and command "stay," flashing the palm of your free hand in front of his face.

3. Step in front of him and act busy while you produce distractions.

4. Return to praise him frequently. Don't allow him to use your praise as an excuse to break the stay, however.

5. If he does anything more than wag his tail or move his head—if, for instance, he tries to scoot forward, rotate his body, or stand up—give the leash a quick upward jerk to return him to the sit. If he doesn't respond, give him two or three jerks. Still no results? Go back to the jerk-and-push combination described earlier in this chapter under "Sit."

6. If he attempts to lie down, tighten up on the leash to stop him and praise him when he stops trying. Loosen the leash and be prepared to repeat this many times over the next week or two.

7. Finally, release him with the "chin-touch okay."

Once he has mastered this procedure, proceed to phase two, the leash-length "sit-stay."

The Art of the Jerk

The jerk is one of the most versatile and important tools in a dog trainer's arsenal. It's used to enforce everything from the "sit," "down," and "come" commands to "off," "drop it," and "quiet."

It is *not* cruel and unusual punishment; in fact, you probably couldn't do any real harm even if you were *trying* to inflict injury—which, of course, you are not. And the automatic obedience that results from using this tool could ultimately save your dog's life.

Your goal is to get his attention quickly and to deliver a correction just strong enough to prevent a repeat occurrence. That said, here's how to do it properly.

- Jerk at the proper time (the moment the dog thinks about pursuing his own agenda rather than yours) and in the proper direction (away from the distraction).
- Deliver the jerk with split-second quickness, so it never chokes, pulls, drags, or nags your dog. Again, your goal is to get his attention, not to injure him.
- Be prepared to deliver several jerks in quick succession, if necessary, if your dog is so mesmerized by a distraction that he doesn't respond to the first one.
- When he turns his attention back to you, make sure you keep it by praising him and directing him back to the task at hand.

In phase one of "sit-stay" training, your dog will learn to remain seated and focus on you despite distractions.

Phase Two

1. Command "stay" as you flash your palm in his face, then walk out to the end of the leash.
2. Teach him that he is to stay put no matter what; do this by moving around, bending down, dropping food or toys and praising him—an excellent distraction.
3. If he moves, don't say a word. Instead, quickly slide your hand up the leash and maneuver him back into the sit with a quick upward jerk.
4. Then return to your "busy" behavior and try again.

When he's mastered the leash-length "sit-stay" in spite of major distractions, move on to phase three, the distance "sit-stay."

Phase Three

1. Tie your longe line to a stationary object, heel your dog to the end of the line, seat him facing away from the stationary object, and attach the longe line to his collar. Leave the leash attached, too.

2. Command "stay" as you show him your palm, then walk away.

3. As you act busy, if he moves, run back to him, grip the leash near the collar with both hands to move him back into his

To teach the distance "sit-stay," first tie your longe line to a stationary object.

Heel your dog to the line, have him sit facing away from the object, snap the line onto his collar along with the leash, and command "stay."

Busy yourself some distance away from him.

original sit position, then give him a quick jerk to encourage
him to stay put. Then don't linger and don't make eye contact, talk to, or touch your dog; instead, return immediately
to your activity.

4. Continue acting busy. When you're done with the exercise,
   return to him, praise him, and release him with the "chin-
   touch okay."

Finally, when he has this down pat even in the face of extreme distractions, you can move on to phase four, the out-of-sight "sit-stay."

Phase Four

Teach your dog to remember your instructions even when he can't see
you by following these steps.

1. Sit your dog behind the corner of a building, command
   "stay," show him your palm, and step out of sight around the
   corner while holding the leash. Although the separation will
   seem great to your dog because he can't see you, it isn't;
   you're maintaining control over him because you're just a few
   steps away and have the leash in hand.

2. Throw distractions, such as toys and bits of food, into his
   view.

3. If he moves, correct him immediately by sliding your hand
   down the leash and jerking his collar upward. Then move out
   of sight again right away and repeat.

4. To make his stay more solid amidst your comings and goings,
   return now and then to praise him, but quickly disappear
   around the corner again. Do this at least three times in a row
   before releasing him with a "chin-touch okay."

Ready for a final exam? Put him in a "sit-stay" while you go about
your normal activities: getting dressed, carrying in groceries and putting them away, making a phone call, even shopping in a busy pet supply store. When he stays without corrections, you can consider this skill
mastered.

To teach the out-of-sight "sit-stay," have your dog sit near the corner of a building and tell him to stay. Then step out of sight around the corner. Add distractions to make him solid in his stays.

"Down-Stay"

Next, teach your dog to stay put in the "down" position for long periods—an especially important discipline for the hyper dog.

Begin by commanding him to lie down and then commanding "stay." Then play groomer with him: Examine his eyes, ears, teeth, paws, and tail. Praise him effusively when he cooperates; use a jerk or jerk-and-push to correct him if he doesn't. Finally, release him with the "chin-touch okay."

When he's obeying you routinely, proceed as you did for the "sit-stay," practicing the "down-stay" with distractions while you're:

1. One step away from him
2. One leash-length away

3. Some distance away from him, with him tied to a stationary object

4. Out of his sight

Off-leash Control

Off-leash training is complex enough to fill an entire volume; and indeed, books *have* been written on this subject. But since so many people move on to this stage without doing any specific off-leash training—thereby courting disaster—we'll cover some basics here.

First, understand that "off-leash training" is a misnomer; the training is done on-leash. You'll want to make sure your dog's responses and understanding are perfect on-leash before removing the leash, because doing so will only magnify any problems he may be having with the leash attached.

Is your dog ready for off-leash work? Test him by setting up the most distracting environment possible: a houseful of guests, or a pet-supply store full of canine customers, for instance. Drop his leash, stepping on the handle to maintain invisible control, and give him the "sit," "down," or "come" command once, without repetition, in a nonthreatening tone of voice. If he obeys, praise him and read on; if he doesn't, pick up the leash and set aside your off-leash plans for the time being.

To begin training for off-leash work, teach him to keep his heel position no matter where the leash is. Hold the somewhat slack leash on your right hand *behind* your back and ask him to heel. If he forges ahead, turn left; if he lags, pat your thigh, praise him enthusiastically, and step ahead while leaving the leash slack. If he meanders away from the heel position, grab the leash with your left hand, place it inside your left thigh, and jump ahead while praising him.

After a few weeks of solid practice, he should walk in the heel position regardless of your speed or direction, and sit automatically around distractions.

But you're far from home free; off-leash control takes time and effort. Until you've achieved it, if you really must go off-leash—for instance, to play Frisbee—and you don't have an enclosed area such as a fenced-in yard or tennis court, at least let your dog drag a 50-foot light line so you have some recourse if he tries to take off. Wear gloves to protect your hands from rope burns if you have to grab the line.

GOOD MANNERS

In addition to the obedience basics just described, you'll want to help your hyper dog learn impeccable manners in and around the house. Keeping an eye glued on him whenever he is roaming free is mandatory until he is solidly trained and trustworthy. The goal is not only to prevent him from soiling or destroying your things; you also want to protect him from deadly pursuits such as chewing on electrical cords and ingesting toxic substances.

Umbilical cording makes it a snap to teach your dog which behaviors are acceptable and which are not.

The trouble with keeping an eye on him is that we humans can be so easily distracted. There are only three solutions: When you can't commit to watching his every move, confine him to a safe, destruction-proof area, put him in a crate, or "umbilical cord" him.

Umbilical cording is, in fact, a great way to bond with a hyper dog while helping him learn his manners. Simply snap on his leash and tie the handle to the left side of your belt. Don't give him too much slack; you don't want your legs to get tangled in the leash.

Nothing fancy—just tie the leash to your belt.

That's all there is to it. Go ahead and do what you ordinarily do. If your dog does anything unacceptable—jumping up, chewing, barking, or trying to relieve himself—you'll be in a perfect position to stop him instantly with a quick pop of the leash.

In and Out

Hyper or not, the well-trained dog graciously accepts crating (as well as other forms of confinement, such as being confined in a room using

To teach your dog to enter his crate on command, position him at the door, one hand on his collar and the other pointing into the crate, and tell him, "kennel up."

Once he's inside, tell him "wait," praise him for cooperating, and use the door bump if necessary to enforce the "wait." Repeat this several times in a row, day after day, and he'll soon enter his crate on command.

a baby gate). That includes entering and leaving the crate or room calmly as soon as you invite him to do so.

It starts with making sure he has a comfortable environment, of course; for tips on turning an ordinary crate into a haven he'll love, see chapter 6. Then teach him to enter the crate on command. Hold his collar, point inside, and tell him "kennel up." Help him in by using your free hand to apply gentle pressure from behind.

Now that he's inside, put one hand on the open crate door and tell him, "wait." As long as he stays put, praise him. If he tries to exit the crate, abruptly bump his nose with the door. Don't close the door on him; your goal is not to injure him but to get him to jump back. If he doesn't, you're not bumping him quickly enough.

When you're ready for him to exit, invite him to do so with a "chin-touch okay," gently touching him under the jaw and saying "okay!"

Repeat this exercise five times in a row, several times a day, until he enters the crate on command.

You can use the same technique to tell your dog to enter and exit other places, from other rooms to the car. For the entry part of it, use the "kennel up" command or—if you're a stickler for accuracy—a phrase such as "get in." Use the "come" command for the exit.

Note that it's *very* difficult to execute a quick, effective, and safe nose bump with standard car, hatchback, or sliding doors. My advice is not to even try it. Instead, perfect your dog's response to the "wait" command using the easily controlled doors in your home. Once he understands, you'll be able to use "wait" successfully in any situation without resorting to the nose bump.

Upstairs and Downstairs

If there are stairs in your life, there will be times when your arms are full of groceries or laundry and you'll want your dog to go up or down the steps well ahead of you—not behind you or at your side, where he may get underfoot.

You can teach this easily by taking him to a flight of stairs and saying "upstairs" while you start to climb and "downstairs" when you're ready to descend. Or simply use a command such as "go on" for either direction. When he races ahead of you, praise him with an enthusiastic "good dog!" After a dozen or so repetitions, he'll be ready to lead the way up or down any flight of stairs.

If you've taught your dog to enter and exit his crate on command, getting in a car should be no problem. You can use the same phrase ("kennel up") or a new one.

Invite him to leave the vehicle with the "come" command.

"Off!"

Want to keep your hyper dog from jumping on everything and everyone in sight? It's not all that difficult. When he starts jumping, simply command "off!" and do one of these four things:

1. If he's jumping on you, knock him off balance by bumping him with your knee.

2. Alternatively, lightly tap on his nostrils with your open palm.

3. If he's jumping on you, someone else, or on furniture or counters and there's a leash attached to his collar, jerk the leash away from the direction he's leaping.

4. If no leash is available, slide your toe sideways under his rear feet or shuffle straight into him until he's no longer interested in having you as a dance partner.

Until he learns not to jump, especially on people, it's a good idea to keep him leashed whenever others are around so you can deliver timely corrections.

Or tap him lightly on the nostrils with an open palm.

One way to stop your dog from jumping up on you is to bump him off balance with a knee.

If he's leashed when he jumps up . . .

. . . simply jerk the leash in the opposite direction.

No leash? Just slide your toe sideways under his rear feet.

Keep Your Weapons Secret

Don't make the mistake of threatening your dog with the Bitter Apple bottle, shaker can, or whatever else you're preparing to use if he doesn't immediately cease his misbehavior. You want him to respect *you*, not a bottle or can.

Instead, wait until he has disobeyed and then deliver the correction quickly, silently, and surreptitiously, hiding the weapon before and after use.

"Quiet"

Although there is some appropriate barking that deserves your praise, many hyper dogs do an awful lot of the other kind of useless and irritating barking. There's no need to let yours develop this bad habit.

Begin by leashing him and then setting him up—creating a situation likely to get him started. That might mean letting him catch sight of another dog, or roughhousing with him, or having a friend ring the doorbell.

The moment he starts barking, command "quiet" and distract him with a sharp jerk of the leash or a quick lip-spritz of a chewing deterrent such as Bitter Apple—a training tool that I highly recommend keeping on hand. Praise him when he is quiet.

If you don't have Bitter Apple spray, hold his collar. Using your other hand, hold his muzzle closed for a few seconds as you jerk the collar until the dog seems to relax. Then remove your hand from the muzzle but continue holding the collar for a minute or so, in case you need to repeat the correction.

After you've done this five or six times, try issuing the "quiet" command by itself, adding the correction only if necessary. If you're some distance away, attach a long leash or line so you can reinforce the command with a quick jerk, if you need to. A spray of the garden hose or a toss of the shaker can may be equally effective.

"Drop It" and "Leave It"

If your hyper dog likes to pick up everything in sight, from socks and shoes at home to cigarette butts and litter on the street, you need to address this behavior. Resist the temptation to pull, rip, or pry his jaws open to retrieve an object. This will make him think that his find is of interest and value to you, too, and he'll either resent your taking it away instead of finding your own, or he'll start bringing you these things as gifts.

Teaching him the "drop it" command is a far better solution. You can even use it in advance of this particular misbehavior, when you see him eyeing something verboten—or add "leave it" to his vocabulary for this situation.

Here's how to teach "drop it."

1. Leash your dog and take him somewhere where he'll be tempted; if necessary, set him up by hiding a smelly food wrapper in a sock or boot. Then, when he picks up a forbidden item, command "drop it" and give his leash a sharp jerk, pulling him toward you.

2. When he has done what you've asked, praise him, back up a few feet, and engage him in a favorite activity—chasing or playing with you, perhaps by enticing him with an acceptable chew toy. To make the contrast even more alluring, dip the chew toy in beef broth before you set him up.

I recently caught my Rat Terrier, Obey, in the act of swiping a child's bunny toy. She ignored my "drop it" command as well as a leash-jerk correction. So I spritzed her lip with the Bitter Apple I keep in a bottle small enough to hide in the palm of my hand.

3. If this doesn't convince him to give his find up, spray your finger with Bitter Apple and touch it to his gum as you issue the "drop it" command—one of the few instances when it's okay to repeat a command. If that still doesn't do the trick, spray Bitter Apple directly on his lip line.

"Leave it" is just like "drop it," except you issue this command *before* your dog picks up a forbidden object. Teach "leave it" using the steps we just outlined, delivering the command and leash jerk microseconds before the dog actually grabs hold of the object.

Shopping

It's a good idea to help your dog learn to distinguish between his toys and everything else. You can do this by tossing a number of personal and paper items on the floor, along with his toys, and then letting him explore. The moment he is about to pick up a taboo item, command "drop it" and jerk the leash away from that item; encourage him to play with the toy.

Don't Eat That

Given a chance, many dogs will eat feces—their own or other animals'. While there's a possibility that a nutritional problem is behind a particular dog's urge (which is why it's worth mentioning to your veterinarian), chances are it's simply behavioral.

The first and obvious step is to prevent this practice by immediately cleaning up after him and keeping him away from other sources of waste. This can nip a bad habit in the bud, before it has a chance to become ingrained.

If it's already too late for that, teach him to be repulsed by it. It's similar to the "drop it" training we've just described, but you're not going to say anything.

Leash him and take him to the area with the waste he prefers. If he goes for it, quickly and silently intervene and spritz Bitter Apple on his lip line. Repeat this with every outing, keeping him leashed and the Bitter Apple handy, until he has refrained from this distasteful practice for at least a week or two.

Don't Roll in That

Some dogs just love rolling in the wonderful smells they find outside. Alas, these smells are often from wildlife dung, which is probably the last scent you want on your dog or in your home.

You can break this habit by taking your dog out on a long line and letting him wander around, sniffing. The moment he begins to lie down for a good roll, give the line a solid jerk or run in the opposite direction and praise him as he follows you.

NURTURING YOUR DOG'S INNER EINSTEIN

Okay, so your dog is not a child and he never will be. But he does have intelligence, and proper schooling can actually increase his IQ. This is true of even the most hyper dogs; in fact, it may be *more* true of hyper dogs than of their laidback cousins.

Keep in mind that dogs learn by doing. With the hyper variety, especially, you'll want to use firm hands and body language to persuade him to settle down, obey, and think.

Applying Your Skills Like a Pro

We've all tasted the difference between scrambled eggs made by an accomplished chef and scrambled eggs made by someone who's never been in a kitchen before. The same ingredients and tools do not necessarily add up to the same flavors, textures, and presentation.

Keep the Right Balance

To help your dog be all that he can be, try to achieve the right balance of work and play, togetherness and detachment.

Remember, first of all, that you're the boss. Of course you cherish him. But he relies on you for everything—food, water, exercise, play, potty breaks. He may think that you were put on this earth solely to serve him. That means you need to be the one to choose the time and place for each of these activities. Don't let him dictate the schedule; learn to distinguish between a real need and a demand for attention.

It also means you need to have a life of your own, and, in turn, give him time to just be a dog—romping in a safe area, playing with other dogs, chewing on toys, and just plain having fun without your involvement.

Learn, too, to distinguish between being bonded and being neurotically attached. The dog freaking out when you leave the house is not a sign of love; it's a sign of neurosis that you'll have to deal with (see Preventing Separation Anxiety, page 115).

Dog training is just the same. Expert trainers know from long experience exactly what tools and techniques to apply to a given task, with what intensity, for what duration, with what timing. And they've learned how to instill excitement and creativity into repetitive exercises that might otherwise become boring.

Don't expect to be able to figure this all out on your own overnight. Give yourself a break and realize that it will take you some time to find what works best for your dog—just as even the world's finest chefs need time to get used to new equipment and ingredients.

If it helps, think of the instructions provided in this book as basic recipes for creating perfect canine behavior. Then adapt them to meet your particular circumstances and your dog's unique personality.

Dog-Wise Communication

Just because your dog is doing well in his training program does not mean he's developed a thousand-word vocabulary. So don't get sloppy with your conversation. For instance, if you want him to sit for grooming, say "sit" and enforce it. Don't string together lots of words into phrases he can't possibly understand. "Come on now, behave yourself and just sit here, will you?" will be nonsense to him.

Don't deliver commands that you are too busy to enforce. If you're chatting on the phone and he's wandering into the kitchen to inspect the counters, don't tell him to "sit" or "come" unless you're going to make him obey; otherwise, he'll learn that this particular command is sometimes meaningless.

Shouting at him is another bad habit—one that will only escalate as he becomes used to each increase in decibel level. Instead, teach him to respond to commands issued in a normal tone of voice and quickly reinforced with a correction.

Repeating commands is another habit to be avoided in almost every situation. You want your dog to consider every word you say to him as extremely important, and to remain alert to you because you're only going to say it once. If he's confused by a particular command, help him understand and obey; if he's just being stubborn, deliver a prompt correction.

Generally speaking, if you know you're unable to reinforce your command at the moment, don't issue it. If you allow him to get away with ignoring a command, you're teaching him something he's better off not knowing.

Using Your Voice

Your voice is a critical tool in training, motivating, and managing any dog—and especially a hyper dog. These dogs are incredibly sensitive to every little vocal variation—not only volume, but how we clip our words, how stern or happy our tone is, whether our inflection conveys calm or excitement.

When we talk about the sequence of command, praise, and release, the tones associated with each step should be distinct—not only to inspire the desired response, but also to help the dog understand, within the context of the task, even if he doesn't quite catch the word you used.

With a command, for instance, your voice should be definite and clipped—but never angry.

Praise, on the other hand, should always reflect great pleasure over a job well done. Pretend you're talking to your best friends. Keep the conversation moving, punctuating your words with giggles, joyous exclamations, and laughter.

Whatever you do, don't drone on and on in a monotone, "good dog good dog good dog good dog good dog" And don't use coaxing phrases like "come on!" Instead, use short, sweet, and enthusiastic phrases, interspersed with silence: "Good boy! (pause) That's it, good,

good, *good!*" And don't linger too long; praise and move on, recognizing your dog's obedience as a momentary event worthy of recognition, with the next event following closely on its heels.

Note that you may have to tone your praise down for an extra-hyper dog, especially if he's quite young. You may even have to put him in a sit-stay before delivering any praise. You'll have to experiment a bit to find out what evokes the best response from your dog.

The release can be nonchalant, simply signifying the end of work. Or it can convey excitement and provoke a mini-celebration on your dog's part: "Good job, pup, let's play for a moment!" might be your underlying message. The signal for it could be the "chin-touch okay" or some other signal. Ideally, you'll use a combination of words and touch, so that there's never any question in the dog's mind if you inadvertently speak the "release" word to someone in normal conversation—never intending to release your dog from his position.

During training, it's best to limit your conversation to commands, praise, and releases, when you have a reason for talking and a point to make. Skip any additional chitchat, or your dog might get bored with the sound of your voice and start tuning you out.

Minimize Touching

If obedience is the goal, less is always more when it comes to touching your dog. Most dogs love to be touched, even when you're delivering a correction, so if you touch him when he disobeys, you may actually be encouraging future disobedience. That's why you'll want to keep touching to a minimum.

To use your hands effectively in training, keep your touch confident, smooth, firm, and as brief as possible. Otherwise your dog will focus on how happy he is that you're touching him and forget about the tasks that you want him to accomplish. Generally speaking, it's better to use the leash to communicate with your dog.

Touching *can* be a good addition to praise, however. Just use your common sense to determine when it's appropriate and when it isn't. For example, there are times when touching would interrupt your work. It would be silly to try to praise him with a touch when you're practicing heeling, changes of pace, turns, and other moving maneuvers.

There are other times when a mild "good job" touch is appropriate—for example, when you've got him in a sit-stay and you want to express your pleasure at his performance, you might want to give him a little scratch behind the ear.

The Shame Factor

Forget trying to manipulate your dog through shame. Dogs don't experience guilt at all; the pained expression they may wear when we berate them is simply the result of confusion and, perhaps, fear.

In fact, shame has no place in human-canine interactions. Instead, keep your corrections short and to the point and redirect your dog to the desired behavior.

Dogs don't experience shame—just confusion and fear. From looking at these expressions, you'd think Justice (right) had been chewing on the book. But the villain in this whodunit was the apparently disinterested Liberty.

With a hyper dog, that may be as far as you can go during a given series of tasks. You'll have to experiment to see what keeps him attentive and obedient, and what sends him over the edge, disrupting the flow of the lesson.

Experiment, too, with what kind of touch elicits the best response in each set of circumstances. Some dogs appreciate a gentle pounding on the chest or side. Others prefer a loin or ear scratch. And still others like a long stroking pet from crown to tail.

Chapter 4

Happy Hour

Fast fixes for releasing hyper energy

··

I t seems we're all busy these days—often too busy to give our hyperactive dogs the attention they want. It's the rare owner who can spend hours each day working every last bit of adrenalin out of his or her hyper dog. In fact, most of us are lucky if we can clear our slates for a couple of good play and exercise sessions per week.

Fortunately, there's good news: We have at our disposal a wide range of high-octane activities to release the hyper dog's pent-up energy quickly and thoroughly, using only as much of *our* energy as we can spare.

It really doesn't matter if you're personally an exercise fiend or count yourself among the world's most highly skilled couch potatoes. You should have no problem developing an energy-release program for your dog that fits your lifestyle—*and* your schedule. In this chapter, we'll take a look at alternatives both popular and obscure.

There's just one thing to keep in mind: The common denominator of all successful programs for hyper dogs is mental stimulation. As hyper dog owner Emily Casey told me recently, "At times my dog can be anxious, whiney, restless, and just generally stir-crazy. I can walk her for several miles and nothing will change. Whereas if I spend fifteen minutes working on obedience commands, she turns into a perfect angel. Go figure!"

THE GREAT OUTDOORS

No matter where you live or what time of year it is, you can provide yourself and your dog with plenty of fresh air while she burns off her excess energy. Here are some idea starters.

Reliable Retrieves

There's something so classic about a good game of fetch, isn't there? Whether your dog prefers a ball or a Frisbee or a favorite stuffed toy, it's one of the most interactive ways for you two to spend a little time together while burning off a ton of her free-floating energy.

Getting Started

If your hyper dog has even a trace of Labrador Retriever in her blood, you already know all there is to know about retrieving. Especially retrieving balls. Especially tennis balls. All I can add to what she has taught you on this important subject is to suggest you consider some of the variations presented here. After all, most retrievers will tirelessly play the same old toss-fetch-return game hour after hour after hour, and even the most devoted dog owner eventually becomes bored.

But if your hyper dog is less inclined toward retrieving, she may need something to pique her interest. Otherwise, you may wind up doing all the fetching—and if you're anything like I was with my first retrieve-resistant pups, feeling like your relationship is not all that it was meant to be.

It's far from hopeless, and most dogs will learn to love retrieving in fairly short order. Simply make a game of it—the kind of game she's already interested in playing.

For instance, you can tap into her competitive spirit by acting like a littermate. Find an object she likes to smell, tease her with it, and toss it out with a flick of the wrist. Hesitate momentarily; if she doesn't go for it, dash toward it gleefully, snap it up, and scamper away, hugging the toy tightly while gloating, "I've got it, you don't!" You'll know you're really thinking like a dog if, after a few sessions, your dog begins snatching up the toy before you can get to it.

That's how we turn dogs who are not Lab-minded into decent, and often keen, retrievers. But even then, there may be

Paunchy Pooch?

It never hurts to ask your veterinarian if vigorous exercise will be safe for your dog—especially if she is overweight or has never done much more than walk around the block. You may be advised to put her on a diet and to increase her stamina gradually. Take both pieces of advice very seriously!

times when your dog merely glances at her favorite ball as it follows a graceful arc away from her. Maybe she's too distracted to retrieve at the moment. If you want her to spring into action, you'll have to first get her attention. Do so by getting silly with her—dancing around her, poking at her gently, laughing, inviting her to chase you. Or, if you prefer a more dignified approach, do a few Sneakaways.

Getting It Back

Once your dog is going after and grabbing the ball, you're halfway home. Now you need to teach her to bring the object of your mutual affection back to you.

No problem: Just snap a long line on her collar before your next toss and, once she's pounced on the prize, use the line to reel her back in, verbally praising her all the way.

Taking Possession

Occasionally, a hyper dog will get it in her head to play "finders keepers," deciding that the idea is to fetch the item and show it to you, but then refuse to give it up. If this describes your dog, follow these suggestions.

First, don't play tug-of-war with her. Your goal is to get her to open her jaws for you, and she won't do that if she thinks this is part of the game. Instead:

1. Reward her for returning with vigorous, two-handed scratching on her back—just above the tail is a favorite spot.
2. Command and enforce the "sit."
3. Put your hand on the ball and say "drop it."
4. If she doesn't respond immediately, blow in her nose.
5. If that doesn't work, spritz a little Bitter Apple on her lip line.
6. As soon as she releases it, praise her and toss the ball again; the chase is her real reward.

Another solution I've heard proposed is to offer to "trade up" to another, even more desirable ball or toy. I'm assuming it works, as long as the dog hasn't committed herself to the item in her mouth for the duration of this play period. But it strikes me as an overly complicated solution, one that invites her to respond to a lure rather than to your command.

If you abhor bribery and prefer a more elegant approach, teach her the "drop it" command.

Catch!

Some dogs take great pride in catching flying objects, such as tennis balls. It's a variation on retrieving that requires excellent hand-eye coordination (your hand, her eyes).

Even if catching is not one of your dog's natural talents, you can help her develop this skill with the popcorn toss—a game that you'll both love. Make a batch of popcorn, apply liberal amounts of butter (okay, this is optional, but it's much yummier this way), and retreat to your favorite spot in the backyard.

Then, alternate: One piece of popcorn for you, one piece for her, with hers launched delicately into the air in a high arc to the sound of a happily delivered word, such as "catch." If you're careful to time this command with the flick of your wrist and opening of your fingers, she'll be catching them like a champ in no time at all—especially if you go after any she lets drop to the ground.

Then just replace the popcorn with a ball large enough that she can't choke on it no matter how determined she is to catch it; she should have to open her jaw fairly wide to accommodate it. Again, say "catch" (or whatever word you've chosen for this command) just as you launch the ball.

You can play this game even in tight spaces, such as on garden paths flanked by your prize roses. And if you have a little bit of room, you can encourage your dog to go deep for long passes—the ultimate in canine catching.

Kickball

If you're not crazy about handling a slimy ball, you can always play kickball with your dog using whatever you have handy—tennis balls work great, although 3.5-inch soft rubber balls are a little easier on your toes, especially in cold weather.

Once she has the basic retrieve down pat, she may drop or toss the ball at your feet, or you may have to use the "drop it" command. Either way, once the ball is waiting at your feet, go ahead and kick it for her.

Some dogs make it their objective to stop the kicked ball from getting past them; they act like the goalie in a soccer match. Others let the ball pass and then take off after it in hot pursuit.

You can vary your footwork to get different results. Aim straight at the ball for a worm-burner (a good way to try to sneak through the legs of a determined goalie). Or use a scooping motion to send the ball into a pretty arc that looks like a miniature Tiger Woods chip shot. To mix it up, surprise your dog by occasionally kicking with one side or another of your foot, thereby sending the ball left or right.

Just one caution: Wear old shoes, because the shoe on your kicking foot is going to look pretty sad after a rousing game.

For a Really Exciting Time

Several devices have been introduced in recent years to make retrieving more exciting than ever. For instance, you can get yourself a Ball Stomp'r, load it with a tennis ball, and stomp on it. It doesn't launch the ball any great distance, but it adds an intriguing new element to the game for retrieve-resistant dogs; some dogs just seem to love the way the ball pops out of this little contraption. With small dogs, take the show inside, using the Stomp'r to launch the ball into corners so that it ricochets off the walls. What fun!

Another highly entertaining tool is the Chuckit! tennis ball catapult, a device that makes it easy to throw the ball great distances without even bending over to pick it up—and, not so incidentally, without touching it.

You can even use an old tennis racket or golf club to do interesting things with a ball. For instance, you can use a golf club to chip it up or down a hill or even across the yard—perhaps over a jump made of soft barriers such as garden clippings or empty boxes. Just don't clobber your dog in the head with it.

Running

What could be simpler than going for a jog with your hyper pooch? Jill Degrave, a student of mine, takes her 90-pound Lab mix, Louie, on five-mile runs almost every day. Sometimes her husband adds another five to this total, and Louie actually ran a total of thirteen miles on one glorious day not long ago. Louie's vet said he's got the best heart she has ever heard, and the exercise definitely makes for a happier and calmer hyper dog.

Most days, Louie runs at least five miles, sometimes more, with owner Jill Degrave.

It's best to use a 2- or 3-foot traffic leash for jogging. That's a leash that looks like a big leather handle with a snap on the end. It's very easy to grip and offers superior control when you want your dog to stay close to you. This way, you can keep your dog on your left side and hold the leash in your left hand, with just your thumb through the loop—an unbreakable grasp when you want to hang on but quickly and easily broken when you don't. Don't ever put your hand all the way through the loop; you have to be able to let go if necessary.

If you are running in the street, run on the left side, facing the traffic, so you can always see what's coming at you and will always be positioned between your dog and the traffic.

Some people do triple duty by going out with their dog and a baby secured in a jogging stroller—a great strategy for parents who find themselves constantly running out of time. Just remember never to hitch your dog to the stroller. Instead, hold the leash in your left hand with your thumb through the loop and any slack in your palm. With this grip, you'll be able to let the dog go instantly if necessary.

Pole Awareness

Whether you're running, biking, or Rollerblading, if you're doing it in the city, street signs will be an issue. You don't want to find yourself bombing along on one side of a pole while your leashed dog is tearing along on the other side.

The solution is to be aware of every pole in your path—and to teach your dog to develop a high level of pole awareness.

You can do this by taking her out on foot and, during the course of conventional training sessions, deliberately weaving in and out of poles. Go ahead and let her get stuck. Then give her the time to figure out how to extract herself, keeping the leash taut. Gradually up your pace until she has learned to stick close to you, and to avoid getting herself stuck in the first place.

Bicycling

Do you have both a bicycle and twenty minutes to spare to exercise your dog, perhaps three times a week? If so, get ready to experience a new level of canine bonding!

You'll have to invest some time up front to show her how to jog contentedly alongside your bike. Begin by walking her on the left side of the bike while you walk on the right side, securing the slightly taut leash in your left hand. That way, you'll be able to use your right hand to steer—and, once you're actually riding, to both maintain your balance and brake.

If at any point she tries to move past the center of the front tire, *abruptly* turn it 90 degrees to the left, directly into her path and perhaps grazing her. She'll dart out of its way—which is why you're maintaining a firm grip on that leash—and most likely not make that mistake again.

As Mark Hersh demonstrates, biking is a great way to give your hyper dog (or dogs) a lot of exercise in a little time. Reserve this activity for sidewalks or streets with low-volume, low-speed traffic.

Once she has learned to stay alongside the bike, repeat the exercise while you're actually riding it in various traffic-free areas—first your driveway, then an alley or quiet cul-de-sac, and finally, lightly traveled streets. If she tries to wander away or to forge ahead of you, give the leash a quick jerk. If necessary, combine the jerk with a momentary turning of the wheel into her path.

One equipment note: In general, I am against using biking shoes or pedal cages when you're biking with a dog. You need to be able to jump off your bicycle in an instant. Anything that prevents you from doing that could have disastrous consequences.

Rollerblading

I admit that I, personally, am terrified at the thought of Rollerblading, with or without my dogs. But I know many owners, experienced Rollerbladers all, who find it a great way to enjoy a favorite sport with their best friend.

When Louie isn't running with Mom and Dad, he enjoys Rollerblading with son Alex Degrave.

If you're an experienced Rollerblader and you have developed solid control over your dog, why not give it a try? Proceed just as you would for jogging: Hold the leash in your hand with only your thumb through the loop. Again, never put your hand all the way through the loop; you need to be able to let go if necessary.

Always start out on a flat surface in low-traffic areas. Save the hills, people and cars for later outings, when your confidence is complete. And avoid these situations until she's learned, through lots of on-foot Sneakaways and extensive obedience sessions, to keep her attention on you and her leash slack even in the presence of distractions.

Horseback Riding

For some of us, nothing comes closer to heaven on earth than riding a well-behaved horse through the woods with a beloved dog trotting on just ahead. It's a perfect Indian Summer day; the air is warm but laced with a crisp undertone foreshadowing the winter ahead. And you're enveloped in the scent of horse and leather and fallen leaves . . .

That's a day in the life of my friend Melanie Moran, who, with her Lab, Luke, and horse, Ray, has ready access to her neighbor's sixty acres, punctuated by cut trails. She says Ray is prone to spook, but when Luke is with them, the horse is much more relaxed. And Luke loves the outings. He chases wildlife and leaps in ponds and in general has a high old time every time they venture out on the trails. She feels closely bonded to him after these journeys, and Luke himself is ready for a good long nap.

Even if you don't have such an idyllic situation, if you have a horse and a place to ride, you can take your hyper dog along for the journey. The only other thing you need is solid off-leash control over your dog, because he won't be wearing any kind of leash or line when you hit the trails.

Luke finds himself happily exhausted after a gallop through the countryside with Melanie Moran and Ray.

Safety First

No activity is 100 percent safe. But a few of those discussed here—specifically running, biking, Rollerblading, and horseback riding—can be risky if you don't take a few precautions. The prerequisite is to have complete control over your dog. This is non-negotiable; to jump into any of these activities with an out-of-control dog is to risk injury to her and to yourself.

Got control? Great! Now give your dog plenty of experience dragging around a fifteen-foot-longe line, so that keeping her legs from getting tangled up becomes second nature to her. At the same time, develop a good understanding of how your dog reacts to surprises, especially surprise encounters with people, other dogs, and wild animals.

If such events normally mean chaos even when she's leashed and you're standing safely on the ground—and if it then takes every ounce of your concentration, cunning, and strength to regain control—you have no business trying to do it from Rollerblades or horseback. Someone is going to get hurt.

If she's not quite *that* out-of-control and you're very, very good at the chosen activity and adept at multitasking, then you're the exception. Inviting your dog into the sport can be a wonderful way to further your training—and hers.

But keep in mind that whether you're running, biking, Rollerblading or horseback riding, you're going to be operating at a higher rate of speed than you would if you were walking. That can either up the danger ante—or reduce it, depending on your dog. If she's in a jogging groove, for instance, she may be oblivious to things that would have been a major-league distraction at a walk.

It also helps to give your dog some practice around horses before going out for a ride. Here's one approach: Spend some time obedience-training your dog in a ring, paddock, or indoor arena where someone is working a horse. This will help her learn to maintain emotional control no matter what the horse is doing.

Next, tie her line to a cinder block or a temporary stake of some sort in the center of the space. Then lead and later ride your horse around her. Finally, try walking them both around on leads.

Your goal is to get them so used to each other that being together is a non-event for both of them. When you've reached that point, proceed to a traffic-safe area, mount up, and have a great time!

This activity is well-suited for sporting breeds such as pointers, retrievers, and spaniels—dogs who are likely to respect your horse's

Specific safety considerations are addressed in the sections dealing with these activities. But please make note of a few general precautions that apply across the board:

- Outings like these represent the one time I prefer to use a retractable leash. When it's locked, even at a short length, it lets you deliver a left-handed jerk emphatic enough to impress your dog to stop, even in the presence of nearly irresistible distractions. It's the next best thing to a Sneakaway when you're on a bike or Rollerblades.
- Avoid pursuing any of these activities on very hot days. Even if you're gliding, your dog will be running.
- If you're bringing along water for yourself, bring some for your dog, too.
- Keep an eye on her energy level. She may be on the way to becoming dehydrated or exhausted but be so excited that she refuses to slow down.
- Don't ever make a hitching post out of anything that can move on its own. That includes everything from bike handles to baby strollers to saddles on the backs of horses.
- Be aware that pavement can be very tough on a dog's joints and—especially if it's hot—on the pads of her feet. If you see any signs of discomfort, stop. If possible, run, ride, or skate on a path flanked by grass, so your dog can run alongside you on a softer, cooler surface. And check her pads after each session until you're confident that she's tolerating it well. If you see a rugburn-like rash, stop for a few days until it heals.

space. Herding breeds may be tempted to nip at the horse's heels and wind up getting kicked. Close herders such as Cattle Dogs and Australian Shepherds are the worst offenders. You may have better luck with a Border Collie, who keeps a greater distance and isn't bred to nip at stock.

Swimming

Swimming is a great way to exercise with a hyper dog—especially if either or both of you has the sort of joint disorders that seem to plague just about every type of creature as we age. In fact, swimming lets you get quite a workout without risking further injury to beleaguered body parts.

If you're fortunate enough to have your own pool or pond, or access to a lake, you're all set—as long as your dog is happy with the idea, of course. Some dogs love swimming and need no encouragement or training; others will have nothing to do with it. Of my first dogs, my Briard couldn't get enough of it. He would swim endlessly around our pond looking like the Loch Ness monster. My Cattle Dog found it mildly entertaining. And my Husky didn't even want to get a toe wet.

If your dog balks, don't throw her into the water or toss her off a boat or pier. Instead, leash her and begin wading in yourself. Keep gentle tension on the leash and tell her "good, good," in a soothing tone of voice. Once she's in deep enough to float, let her paddle a few strokes and then allow her to return to shallower water so she can get her footing again. Gradually increase her paddling time. If you're in a pool, lead her back up the stairs early on, so she'll know how to get out. And either way, if you choose to swim with her, I recommend that you both wear life jackets.

It's true that some dogs will never enjoy this activity. But if you're into water sports, you should be able to persuade her to at least tolerate it, and not to panic if she gets dunked unexpectedly. Eventually, she may really surprise you.

Of course, not everyone is fortunate enough to have access to the right swimming spot. If you don't but would really like to swim with your dog, check with your local veterinarian, dog club, and animal shelter; there may be businesses nearby that are quietly catering to human and canine swimmers. And call your county park system to find out if they ever open their pools to dogs and their owners.

Photographer Adam Senatori's Labrador Retriever loves—you guessed it!—swimming and tennis balls.

Tire-pulling

If your dog is tireless and you're short on everything from cash and time to space and energy, tire-pulling may be a satisfying solution for both of you. Begin by outfitting her with a weight-pull harness, available online or in catalogues. Let her get used to wearing it while you're around to supervise.

At the same time, pick up a small, cart-sized tire and put an eye bolt in the middle of a tread. Let your dog get used to having it around. Next, attach a heavy-duty line to the tire bolt. Start out with a 15-foot line if your dog is sound-sensitive or might be worried by the tire; otherwise, a 6- to 10-foot line is fine.

Now attach a leash to the harness ring, lead your dog up to this strange assembly, and let her sniff around while you praise her profusely. Hook the line up to the harness ring, too, and lead your dog forward with the leash. As she reaches the end of the line, she will have to pull the tire. Use more praise, as well as treats or squeaky toys if necessary.

Start slow. Begin with a few sessions of 15 to 20 feet for the first few days and gradually work up to longer distances and bigger tires. It's also a good idea to begin by working on grass or dirt, to muffle the sound. Eventually, you'll be able to work on a sidewalk, so that even a short walk around the block will satisfy her spunk quota for the day.

Backpacking and Hiking

What could be better than a day spent on the trails with your best friend at your side—unless it's adding a night or two of camping to the mix?

There are obvious hazards on some hiking trails, of course, and you'll want to use common sense when you consider your route. Wildlife could be a threat, especially with a smaller dog; in some parts of the country, coyotes, foxes, and wolves have become bolder in recent years. So you'll want to remain alert.

Other dogs could also become a threat, especially if you're entering their territory. Be willing to alter your route, if necessary. If there's no time for that—if, in fact, an angry dog is already approaching you— try the advice in the box on page 88.

Snow Sports

Having an excuse to curl up together in front of a roaring fire is one of the perks of dog ownership in the north. But it's certainly not your only alternative for canine bonding through the long, cold winters. You can also pick up a little equipment and make the most of all that snow.

If an Angry Dog Approaches

Unless you never leave the house with your pooch, sooner or later you'll have an unpleasant encounter with a territorial and angry dog.

The best defense is having a well-controlled dog on the other end of your leash. Quickly put her into a sit-stay and position yourself between her and the approaching dog. Your objective is to block the approaching dog's view of your dog and to present yourself as an insurmountable obstacle to his desires.

Then—quickly, before he charges—point your finger off into the distance and curtly tell him "go back!"

One caution: When it's cold out, we tend not to think about dehydration. But it's just as much a threat in winter as it is in summer, and we need to be aware of the extra workout that running through the snow gives our dogs. Even if you aren't bringing water along for yourself, bring some for your dog if you're going to be out for an hour or more.

Snowshoeing

If you can walk, you can snowshoe. It doesn't require expensive equipment. In fact, used modern or antique snowshoes can be found online, in classified ads, or at used equipment shops. Although you can't execute a Sneakaway on snowshoes, if you've taught your dog basic obedience skills, you should be ready to share very enjoyable winter hikes. And you'll both get a great workout for your efforts!

Cross-country Skiing

If you enjoy this sport and have good off-leash control over your dog, why not take her

Lisa Ruesch and her Labrador Retriever, Tess, enjoy spending Wisconsin winter days snowshoeing.

along the next time you head out? Dashing through the snow will provide her with an excellent cardiovascular workout.

Skijoring

Up for more excitement? If your hyper dog weighs at least 30 pounds, consider skijoring—an adaptation of cross-country skiing in which your dog supplies the power, pulling you across the snow at sometimes exhilarating speeds!

You don't need much in addition to your basic cross-country skiing gear to participate in this increasingly popular sport. Just wrap a skijoring belt around your waist, outfit your dog with a basic sled-dog racing harness, attach yourselves to each other with a towline, and you're all set. In fact, you can hook yourself up to two or three dogs at a time, if you wish.

Just about the only prerequisite is that you have good skiing skills. And since by now you should have trained your dog not to lunge ahead of you when walking on a leash, you'll have to do a little preparatory training to encourage her to go ahead on command, under this very limited set of circumstances. For tips, check out the Sledding section in chapter 8.

THE INSIDE STORY

You don't have to head outside to give your hyper dog a workout. Choose one or more of the following activities, or make up your own games. A good time will be had by all!

Retrieving Revisited

Okay, so you probably aren't going to want to toss a tennis ball around your house, especially if it's a game that really excites your dog. But you *can* satisfy her retrieving instinct and need for a high-octane workout by taking advantage of any stairs in your house. Simply launch a ball or other toy up or down the stairs and let her do what comes naturally— or, if necessary, follow the steps outlined on page 76 to develop a retrieving instinct where none seems to exist.

Don't worry about overexerting her. The game will be self-limiting; when she gets tired, her interest will wane and she'll retire to her favorite corner.

One note of caution: If your stairs are slippery, consider installing nonskid pads or a runner before inviting your dog to chase up or down them—especially if she'll be racing downstairs and if she considers fetching her raison d'être. Or shorten the distance by starting on a landing or in the middle of the staircase.

Rapid-fire Commands

Rapid-fire Commands are a great way to combine obedience training with a fast workout for your dog. Described in chapter 10, they're also excellent for quickly suppressing over-exuberant canine greetings when company arrives.

The primary reason this technique works so well is that it's mentally stimulating for your dog, and that can do more to relax a hyper dog than an hour of mindless exertion. One of my students—a high-school student with a fun-loving but demanding Yorkie-Poo—reports that her dog often caps off three minutes of rapid-fire commands with a three-hour nap.

Stalking, Chasing, Pouncing, and Playing

Sometimes the most exciting thing in a dog's world can be an owner who gets just as silly as she feels. So go ahead: Attach a leash so you can enforce commands. Then get down on her level and get goofy!

- Stalk her the way a cat stalks a mouse.
- Leap out and pounce at her.
- Use eye contact and lurching movements to get a game of tag going.
- Toss a ball and try to beat her to it, gloating excessively if you succeed.
- Tease her with her favorite toy.
- Challenge her to a race—if necessary, rearranging your furniture to create a straightaway, oval track, or slalom course.

Then, without a moment's notice, toss some obedience commands into the mix. Your goal is to have fun with your dog without losing control of the situation.

The Blanket Caper

This one's easy: Grab an old blanket, sneak up on your dog, throw the blanket over her, and laugh as she runs around trying to escape it. Although most dogs find this great fun, this variation on a pounce is not for every dog. Don't try it if you think it will make yours freak out.

Play During Training

One of the best ways to make learning fun for your dog is to make play a key part of your training sessions. That's as true inside the house as it is in the great outdoors.

Your goal with this "controlled play" is to develop and refine her on/off switch. This will enable you to:

- Build rapport with her
- Gain control even when she's feeling extra hyper
- Teach her to respond to commands without any warm-up

So go ahead, put her through her paces, practice commands new and old, and punctuate the session with frequent bursts of rollicking good times—running, hiding, pouncing, playful nudging, light scratching, whatever delights your dog. When she begins losing control, return to the commands.

Hide and Seek

Was this one of your favorite games as a child? It still can be, whether you're "it" and the pursuer is a beloved hyper dog, or vice versa.

The most obvious way to play this game is to tell your dog to stay while you leave the room, hide, and give one short "come" command. But there are variations that are equally fun and give you the added pleasure of watching her search.

For instance, if you have a partner handy, such as a son, keep your dog with you while he runs off to hide. Then stand up and ask your dog, "Where's Johnny?" as you look around yourself. If your dog is stumped, Johnny can provide a clue or two by calling her name. Her reward for discovering the hiding place, of course, includes excited squeals and generous pets.

You can also play hide and seek with a favorite toy—preferably one that you've given some sort of name, so you can ask after its whereabouts. Tiny treats will also work. Even a non-sporting dog will enjoy that sort of hunt! Or you can turn the tables and sneak up on a dog who is quietly waiting for you.

Wacky Recalls

This exhilarating, entertaining, and educational game will improve your dog's recall more dramatically than any other single technique. To begin, get your dog's attention with a sharp clap, barking "hey!" or calling "come"—or doing all three. Then praise her uproariously as you

Shadow, one of my canine students, loves doing the conga with "his" kids, Erin (center) and Jenna, as they snake their way through the house to their favorite tunes.

race down the hall, up the stairs, and duck into a dark corner of your study (or wherever your house allows you to race to and hide).

Hyper dogs will celebrate the game by jumping on your head and lavishing you with kisses—if they don't first knock you over as you try to run away. If you remember to do a wacky recall 25 percent of the time when you call your dog, she'll race to you every time she hears "come."

Tug-of-War

I don't ordinarily recommend playing tug-of-war with a dog, because it can encourage possessiveness and teach her not to relinquish items to you—including personal belongings and potentially dangerous items. Tug-of-war has also been known to encourage dominance or aggression in certain individual dogs.

Still, it's a game that dogs naturally enjoy, so learn how to play it responsibly. Do so by injecting a note of discipline every once in awhile: In the midst of a tug, give your dog a command to sit or lie down or heel—and enforce it.

If the game gets out of hand, put a stop to it quickly with a series of obedience commands.

Watch Your Manners—and Hers

It's fine to get your dog good and riled up with any of these games, but don't let her cross the line—and don't cross the line yourself. Men, in particular, will often growl and wrestle aggressively with a dog, in the process succeeding only in frightening her—or in teaching her that it's cool to threaten and play rough.

Nip any unacceptable behaviors in the bud. If vigorous play leads to any sort of biting or growling, leash your dog before you begin. Then, the moment she engages in an unacceptable behavior, give her something positive to do instead—sitting, lying down, staying, and coming, for example—and use the leash to enforce your commands.

Then return to your game. Keep substituting positive commands whenever necessary, until she understands that having fun is not a license to misbehave.

TWICE THE FUN

You are undoubtedly your dog's favorite person in the world—next to the kids next door and Uncle Ben and Grandma Joan and whoever else just happens to walk into the room.

In short, your dog's list of favorite people may be as long as the list of people she knows. And if she is overjoyed simply spending time with you, just imagine how delirious she will be if she gets to play with two or more people simultaneously!

You might try hitting tennis balls back and forth between you and a friend, letting her retrieve the misses for you. Allow her to help your kids practice pitching and catching a softball. Or invite her to play roller hockey with them in the driveway.

You can inject some learning into the fun. For example, improve her recalls by attaching two retractable leashes to her collar. Give one reel device to a friend and keep one yourself. Take turns calling your dog, alternately letting the line out and reeling her in.

You can also extend your play invitations to a friend with a dog, in the process giving your hyper dog a much more intensive workout. If you're not a terribly serious runner, for example, but have good off-leash control over your dog, you can triple the amount of exercise she gets by inviting a buddy with a dog to join you. Simply head for a traffic-safe area, unleash the pooches, and go for a nice jog. They'll rack up three times your mileage as they frolic with each other along the way.

THE SOCIABLE DOG

Dogs are pack animals. They enjoy spending time with others of their own species. So why not give them a chance to do so once in awhile . . . or even every day?

Galloping along a sandy beach with her best friend—what more could a hyper dog want out of life?

Play Groups

A play group is any kind of a by-invitation-only get-together for your dog. It may be carefully planned, or organized on the spur of the moment.

Setting up a play group is as simple as arranging a play date for a child. If there are some neighborhood dogs whom you like—and whose behavior you admire—talk to their owners and suggest getting together regularly for rousing doggie play.

Or you can form an impromptu play group if you happen across a dog who seems to be the right speed for yours. Biking through a park recently with my two small dogs jogging alongside me, I noticed a fellow with an adorable Weimaraner puppy on a leash. I stopped and asked if he'd like his dog to play with mine. He agreed, so we let them tear around together off leash. My oldest, Able, kept the other two close by and under control, and they all had a wonderful fifteen-minute romp.

Another option is to take your pooch to a local Yappy Hour—an organized play group sponsored by a local dog-related business, such as a dog day care center, kennel, pet shop, or training studio. It may be free or there may be a nominal charge per dog, but you can rest assured that there will be professionals in attendance to keep everything under control. Check your local newspaper or look online for the Yappy Hour nearest you.

Dog Parks

I like the fact that organized play groups enable me to know everything I want to know about the health, temperament, and training of my dogs' canine companions. Alas, that's nearly impossible at big-city dog parks, where parasites and viruses may be present in abundance, and where some dogs are so aggressive that they won't let the neutral nature of the territory stop them from trying to dominate every dog in sight.

Dog parks can also bring out the worst in even a fairly well-trained dog, if she's allowed to run at will. If there's no balance between controlled obedience and uncontrolled play, her natural impulsiveness will be encouraged and her adrenalin levels may rise until you have a tough time bringing her back under control. At the very least, this chain of events can make a hyper dog even more hyper—definitely not the outcome most owners expect from a romp in the park.

Nevertheless, dog parks do have a number of advantages, and I know many enthusiastic dog-park boosters who take their dogs to them nearly every day without incident. Here, the dogs are allowed to run and play with the other canines, in the process burning off energy they might otherwise have applied to chewing, chasing, and, in general, making pests of themselves at home.

What's more, dog parks usually present a golden opportunity for working on your dog's obedience in the presence of otherwise irresistible distractions. Practice walking her on a loose leash, for instance, using Sneakaways whenever necessary to enforce the heel. Do Rapid-fire Commands. Attach a light line and enforce a series of commands from a distance. If you can strike the right balance between training and play for your dog's particular needs, some time spent at the dog park may turn out to be one of the best things you've ever done for her.

If you weigh the risks against the benefits and decide that a dog park is a good option for you, look for one with an active and vigilant user group—usually dog-owner sponsors who police the site, stepping in to encourage leashing or ejection of aggressive dogs (not to mention prompt clean-up of waste).

Dog Day Care

This is the latest trend in cities large and small, where growing numbers of busy owners have signed their hyper dogs up for day care services. It's a great idea—in theory, anyway.

The trouble is that the execution can be so flawed that a few weeks at one dog day care center can turn a hyper dog into a monster—although a few weeks at a really good center can transform a troublesome pup into a perfect lady.

I've talked with countless owners who've experienced both kinds of dog day care, and the difference seems pretty clear: the presence of a training component. Owners who use day care that includes training rave about what the experience has done for their dogs.

"Harley is so much calmer and more obedient when he comes home from day care," the owner of a young Rottweiler told me recently. "I'm sure it's because of the training he gets, along with the constant supervision. He doesn't have a chance to pick up bad habits."

These comments are typical. So, too, are the reports I hear from many new obedience-class students who've experienced the other sort of dog day care—the sort that is nothing more than a nine-hour free-for-all from which their dogs have emerged either out of control, cringing from having been picked on all day by a bully, or in firm possession of horrid new housetraining habits.

If you're thinking of day care for your hyper dog, look for a center that includes training. It's obviously a key component at Todd Thurber's Come Sit Stay and Play in Greenfield, Wisconsin (www.comesitstayplay.com), as these regulars prove.

Before enrolling your dog in a day care program, be sure to check it out thoroughly. Observe the center at different times during the day, if possible, to see what sort of supervision the dogs get. If you see mayhem, uncorrected bullying or barking, or soiling indoors, look elsewhere.

On the other hand, if you see a steady succession of training sessions—either with individual dogs or small groups—consider it a good sign.

But don't stop there. Find out what kind of training method is used to see if it gels with your thoughts on the subject. At the very least, talk with some other owners and find out if their dogs seem to be better behaved when they've been in day care, or when they've stayed home. Ask the owners about their dogs' impulsiveness, emotional control, and adrenalin levels, and how day care affects these variables.

Is *some* day care better than none at all? Not necessarily. Personally, if I couldn't find a place that exercised my dog's mind and spirit as well as her body, and used training techniques I agreed with, I would keep her at home. I would then commit myself to spending a chunk of concentrated time each evening on obedience training and playing with her.

Chapter 5

Winding Down

From flat out to flat down in minutes

···

N ow that you know how to control your hyper dog and how to unleash his energy for quick burnoff, you'd probably like to know how to put the brakes on all that hyperactivity. This is a legitimate concern with hyper dogs, some of whom just don't know when to quit. Even after hours of activity, they're still going strong and can't quite hide their frustration over your laziness. This can be annoying if you two are alone, embarrassing if you're with others, and downright dangerous if someone fragile, such as an elderly person or a toddler, enters the picture.

What's the secret to calming down an excited hyper dog? Provide him with an even more attractive and highly soothing distraction— perhaps one described in this chapter.

GOOD GROOMING

For most of us women (and perhaps more than a few of you men), there's nothing more relaxing than an hour or two in a spa, being pampered by a staff whose sole purpose is making you feel good and look great. The good news is that, armed with just a few basic tools, you can provide your hyper dog with much the same experience in a fraction of the time—and without spending a dime!

In fact, grooming is one of the best ways to calm and bond with a hyper dog. Plan to do a thorough grooming weekly, and partials whenever the need or mood arises. Here's how.

Use your free hand to hold your dog's collar, if necessary. Start with a good brushing, concentrating on the areas that obviously give him a leg-thumping good time. Move on to the often-neglected areas that mat or collect dirt—his face, neck, rear, and underbelly. Brush his teeth using a meat-flavored doggy toothpaste. Trim his nails and clean his ears. And take this opportunity to check him out thoroughly, feeling for lumps or bumps that might warrant a look by your vet.

Need help with any of these steps? Consider taking him to a professional groomer or breeder and asking for lessons and equipment advice. Consult a breed-specific book. Or check out a dog grooming guide or web site.

Guest Etiquette

Sometimes helping a dog wind down means preventing him from getting wound up in the first place. It's most obviously an issue when guests arrive and make a big fuss over your hyper dog. All that excitement and attention can be more than even the most painstakingly trained dog can bear.

The solution? Put your dog's needs first.

That means you need to do two things before your guests arrive. First, ask them to totally ignore him for the first fifteen minutes of their visit. Second, snap a leash on him before you open the door, so you can correct him if necessary.

Once your guests have arrived, invite them to move around freely, since a hyper dog is less likely to glom onto a moving target.

If they can't resist (and who can blame them?), admit that you've been having trouble with your dog becoming overexcited with guests and ask them to treat the visit as your opportunity to train him. Excuse yourself and do some quick Sneakaways, interspersed with Rapid-fire Commands. By the time you're through, he will be calm—or at least a lot more composed than he was a few minutes earlier.

In the meantime, you can begin alleviating this problem by treating your own homecomings as nonevents. Act oblivious to your dog, ignoring him and his shenanigans completely for the first fifteen minutes.

If he leaps on you, don't yell at him; it will only inflame his excitement. And don't push him away; he'll see that as a game. Instead, focus on some other activity—chores or changing your clothes, for instance. If he gets in your way in an attempt to engage you in play, stumble into him relentlessly. Or, if he needs to be fed or walked, do so without emotion.

When the fifteen minutes are up, have a ball: wrestle, play, cuddle, do whatever makes you both happy.

If your dog fidgets, try setting him on a platform that puts him at a comfortable height for you. Select one with a surface area small enough to keep him from getting happy feet. If he refuses to stand still, hold his collar and let him experience gravity for a split second: Let him step off the edge of the table if he insists on doing so, rescuing him after a nanosecond of panic sets in but long before all four feet leave the table. That should adjust his attitude about staying put, freeing him to relax and enjoy all the pampering.

DOGGIE MASSAGE

Why stop with grooming? With a little common sense, you can treat your hyper dog to a massage. Once you've used this technique a few times to relax your dog, he'll most likely drop everything at the sound of the word "massage." Here's how to ensure it.

For your first session or two, pick a time when your dog is already relaxed and content—perhaps when he's stretched out on your couch or bed (if he's allowed there). Even if it doesn't make any difference to him, it might be more comfortable for you. And you won't have to use any restraint to get started.

One of our most experienced doggie masseurs advises beginning with light, gentle touches on the paws or ears before moving to other parts of the body—perhaps to the shoulders, since they bear the brunt of the work each day. Gently massage them, one at a time or simultaneously, applying a bit more pressure if he seems to be enjoying the attention.

Next, slowly run your fingers down each side of his backbone, massaging from the base of his neck down past his shoulders. Then position the palms of your hands on his upper back and very slowly and gently massage all the way down to his tail.

Finally, turn your attention to his head, stroking his cheeks with a feather-light touch.

Just how effective is massage at turning a hyper dog into the picture of peace? "My dog loves massage so much, I often fear that she will melt right into the floor," says an Australian Shepherd owner I know. "It's very calming for her and has an immediate effect."

If you want, you can add comforting music to your massages—ideally, music you sing yourself, with your dog's name thrown into the lyrics frequently. (One of the most wonderful things about our dogs is that they love our lullabies, even if we can't carry a tune.)

Massage Do's and Don'ts

To make your doggie massages irresistible, follow these guidelines:

- *Do* be gentle. You're stronger than you think.
- *Don't* ever press on your dog's abdomen.
- *Do* be especially careful around his head.
- *Don't* try to massage away an injury; take him to the vet.
- *Do* consider buying a book on canine massage to get the most out of this bonding experience.

Many variations on canine massage have been developed over the years. Some owners swear by specific approaches not only to calm hyperactivity, but to solve an enormous range of problems.

If you want to get technical, pick up a book on doggie massage; there are a number of good ones available.

Whatever the technique, massage is almost universally adored by our canine friends. Why? Perhaps, as some experts say, because it stimulates circulation and releases blocked energy. Or maybe it just relaxes overworked muscles. Whatever the reason, if it soothes your dog's mind, by all means, continue.

SNUGGLING AND SNOOZING

Another great way to relax a hyper dog is to chill out with him yourself; snuggle up together on the floor or couch or invite him to take a nap with you.

Yes, a nap *in your bed*. I know lots of well-adjusted, perfectly trained dogs, hyper and otherwise, who regularly sleep with their owners. With most dogs, there's nothing wrong with it. There are just two exceptions.

First, if your dog refuses to leave when you tell him to or has serious behavior issues such as house soiling, biting, or guarding items or territory, don't invite him up on any furniture. You want to reduce his impulsiveness, not encourage it. Do your cuddling with him on the floor.

Second, if another human objects to having a dog in bed, it's my strong recommendation that you respect that objection. Human relationships really *should* take precedence over our relationships with our dogs, after all, and some people are convinced that dogs have no place in human beds. For a compromise that should make everyone happy, check out chapter 6.

Heal Thyself

"Generally speaking, if I'm busy, she's busy," a student of mine said recently of her dog. "And if I relax, she'll try to relax."

There's wisdom in this observation, because a hyper dog will often reflect the mood of those around him. If your household is tranquil, your dog is likely to be relatively tranquil. If it's frenetic—and especially if its pace is matched by a great deal of drama or noise—your hyper dog is much more likely to reflect the excitement by bouncing off the walls.

In other words, if your dog remains hyperactive even after training and exercise, take a close look at the environment you've created for him. You may both benefit from more peaceful conditions.

But if these aren't issues for you, why pass up this unique bonding experience? Former student Rose Pickering may have described it best in talking about her Dandie Dinmont Terrier, Lloyd. "I feel most bonded with him when I wake up in the morning and see those brown eyes, that goofy yawn, and hear that thwacking tail on the quilt. Then he scooches up toward me, paw over paw, to give me a quick cuddle-up before we hop out of bed."

As noted earlier, the "down" position is inherently relaxing for a dog. When you join him, although his joy will at first know no bounds, it will soon be replaced by total relaxation.

Teaching him to get up on the couch or bed should be a piece of cake, even if you've previously discouraged him from climbing onto the furniture. Simply leash him, lead him to the couch or bed, pat it encouragingly, command "up," and praise him profusely when he complies. If necessary, use the leash to lead him up; this will give a reluctant dog the extra assurance he needs to know that you *really* want him on the furniture.

Once he jumps up on command (I give him about six seconds to get the idea), go through the same process while you're sitting on the bed, and finally, while you're lying down.

The bigger challenge will be getting him to jump *off* when you've decided it's time for him to vacate the premises—which you'll want to do if he's hogging the bed or repeatedly standing up, circling, and burrowing in the bedding, or if his snoring is keeping you awake. Don't simply push him off; a hyper dog is bound to think that you're offering him a rousing game of Let's Shove Each Other Until We've

Laughed Ourselves Silly. Instead, work on it with him at some point; leash him and stand next to the couch or bed. Command "off," moving away from the bed and giving his leash just enough of a jerk toward the floor to make your intentions clear. Praise him as he responds—even if you *are* providing much of the muscle. Repeat this exercise several times in a row. Once he has become proficient at the "off" while you're standing, sit on the couch or bed and repeat the "off/jerk/praise" process several times. Finally, lie down and repeat.

If you want to improve your dog's understanding of furniture etiquette—for instance, so that he'll understand he may jump up only when he's been invited—place enticing toys on the floor. Within a session or two, you'll have at the ready a perfect way to get even a thoroughly wound-up hyper dog yawning contentedly.

Essential Oils

I've had some owners tell me that their hyper dogs have been de-stressed to some extent by essential oils and flower remedies (sometimes called Bach flower remedies) used in conjunction with solid basic training—that is, training that results in one-command control around distractions and temptations of all types.

Essential oils and combination products such as Rescue Remedy, which are made primarily from distilled plants, are available at health food stores and some pet supply shops. They can be administered by hand, dropper or atomizer, or by putting a few drops on your dog's blanket. Various formulations are recommended to address specific problems, including those related to stress and anxiety.

Do they work? Well, these distillations *have* been used for centuries, and in recent decades studies have confirmed at least some of the benefits claimed for them. I personally had a curling-iron burn on my face that healed almost instantly thanks to an essential oil product, and I know of a very ill woman with a compromised immune system who used something similar to obtain fast relief from a stubborn rash. Is it too much of a stretch to think these products might deliver some emotional healing, as well?

If you're intrigued, I encourage you to give it a try.

Better Living Through Chemistry

Let me say up front that I don't approve of putting a hyper dog on drugs as a first resort in trying to calm him down. Not even as a ninth or tenth resort.

You Be the Judge

If you search diligently for ways to settle down your hyper dog, you'll probably find scores of self-proclaimed cures out there—many at least a little out of the mainstream. For instance:

- A tight T-shirt or ace bandage wrapped snugly around his chest and body has been said to have a calming effect.
- Holistic, homeopathic, and doggie chiropractic medicine experts suggest techniques ranging from dietary changes and stress-reduction regimens to physical manipulations.
- Various specialty diets have been designed to adjust the type and amount of protein a dog ingests or to eliminate the chemicals that are allegedly making him hyper.
- Nutritional supplements containing various vitamins or herbs will alleviate anxiety-related behaviors, according to their manufacturers.
- Reiki "energy healing" is said to work because it channels "universal life energy" via your hands, which are uncannily guided to the parts of your dog's body in greatest need of such nourishment.
- Acupressure is said to affect energy levels—in this case, balancing or releasing them—working wonders on the recipient's health, digestion, and emotional well-being.
- Mood CDs can relax your dog or help him overcome his fear of a sound such as thunder, according to those who sell them.

Do these remedies really work, or is it simply that when we administer them, we end up giving our dogs more compassion, concern, and attention? I don't know the answer to this question, but clearly a hyper dog will get some level of relief just from receiving a higher level of care.

That said, it's true that some people swear by remedies such as these. Others who've tried them say they were not impressed. All I can suggest is that you give any that appeal to you (and your pocketbook) a try.

But be especially wary of anything that involves dietary changes. Your dog should be on a top-quality diet, which is readily available in the premium food section of any pet supply store (or in your own kitchen, with the proper ingredients and recipes, carefully followed). Check with your veterinarian before making any faddish changes to your dog's diet.

However, once all other alternatives have been exhausted, certain individual dogs may find needed relief with drugs such as antidepressants, used in conjunction with exercise, socialization, and sound basic training.

One of my assistants at Amiable Dog Training, a supremely level-headed owner/trainer, had a Beagle. No matter what she did, the dog experienced horrible, debilitating separation anxiety whenever she left him. None of the usual or even unusual remedies helped him much, nor did a spin with Rescue Remedy.

Finally, in desperation and with her veterinarian's careful supervision, she turned to Prozac as a last resort. The difference was dramatic. After a while, she tried taking her dog off the drug, but the improvements disappeared. So she started it up again and kept the dog on it for the rest of his life.

No responsible vet will prescribe such an expensive and frequently ineffective pharmacological approach without also recommending serious obedience training and environmental changes. And with good reason: Studies have shown that the drugs are virtually useless unless they're administered in conjunction with sound behavior-modification strategies.

Chapter 6

Feng Shui

Creating a safe haven for your hyper dog

··

F
eng shui is the ancient Chinese art of creating a space that enhances the inhabitants' health and happiness—just the ticket for anyone whose responsibilities include taking care of a hyper dog. And why not? We all want our hyper dogs to have peaceful, comfortable homes in which stressors have been reduced to an absolute minimum, homes where they're free to rest and play in comfort while human traffic flows quietly past.

This can be accomplished even under serious space constraints. In my compact condo, for instance, I take full advantage of every spare inch. For at-home grooming, I had a simple collapsible table built at a comfortable height for me. I keep my dog supplies (from shampoo, grooming tools and medications to training equipment, jackets, food, and toys) within easy reach on a lazy Susan in a cupboard. And my dogs have a choice of beds—a wrought-iron model tucked into a walk-in closet, a cushy blanket snuggled onto the bottom shelf of a built-in cabinet, and a comfortable crate that provides a window view of a neighboring rooftop.

CREATURE COMFORTS

If we're getting the rest we need, we humans spend the largest single chunk of our lives in bed, sleeping. Dogs are no different, except that, compared to us, they're Olympic-caliber snoozers, sleeping, on average, eighteen hours a day. It makes sense, then, that when we think about creating a comfortable home environment for them, we should begin with their sleeping accommodations.

The Crate: A Home Within Your Home

Some owners think crating a dog is cruel and unusual punishment. But properly used, nothing could be further from the truth. In fact, many dogs love their crates so much that they'll climb in for a rest whenever nothing more exciting is going on—when they could jump up on the couch or your favorite chair. So even when your dog has earned her freedom around the house, make it a point to either leave the crate door open for her or remove the door entirely; she'll appreciate it.

How do you go about setting up the best crate for your dog? Make sure you consider all the following points:

- Size
- What it's made of
- What's inside
- Where the crate is placed
- In-crate entertainment
- Introducing the crate properly
- Teaching your dog to enter and exit on command

Size is the first important consideration. Select a crate that's large enough to allow your dog to stand up, stretch, and turn around. If she's still a puppy, buy a crate big enough to accommodate her when she's grown; in the meantime, you can make it fit her current proportions by blocking off the back with a heavy-duty cardboard box or something similar. This will give her cozy quarters that she will resist soiling—an excellent housetraining tool.

Material is the next factor. I strongly recommend solid plastic or wire mesh, whichever you prefer; most dogs seem to have no particular preference. There are some attractive alternatives out there today, including lovely rattan models, but chewing can be an issue with these crates, and ingesting parts of her crate could seriously harm your dog. If she chews at all, resist the temptation.

There are also mesh- or nylon-covered crates that are wonderful for traveling, as long as you'll be there most of the time to supervise the dog. But don't leave her alone for long in one of these; given enough time, she may well figure out how to unzip the door or dig or chew her way through the fabric. Besides, in any environment other than your home or car, a canvas crate will not protect her from dangers such as other animals.

Toys such as these are good options for safe chewing, whether or not your dog is confined.

If you choose wire mesh for your at-home crate, go for a heavy gauge and pick the one with the most connectors or fasteners holding it together. Yes, more connectors will make it more of a job to fold down for storage, but they will also make it tougher for a determined dog to escape. There are many good brands available today; Central Metal is one I've personally used and recommended for many years.

Whatever the outside material, make the inside as comfortable as possible without introducing dangerous materials. By all means provide bedding, but if your dog chews it up, you'll have to remove it and let her sleep on the bare crate bottom.

Crate placement can be the key to contentment. Set it up it in the room where you spend the most time—ideally, in the spot she seems to favor, such as a sun-washed (but not baking hot) corner out of the way of the traffic flow.

Unfortunately, your favorite room can also be the tightest on space. You may need to be creative.

Say, for instance, that you spend most of your waking hours in a small home office. Putting the crate under your desk might be ideal—except that it will probably be awfully dark. One solution is to place a mirror between the crate and the wall. I did that for Obey when I first brought her home, and she enjoyed not only the light but also the stimulation provided by gazing at herself and at the activities reflected in the mirror. Another option is to turn your dog's crate into a table or even a shelf by setting it on the floor or a filing cabinet and adding a stylish top.

Leave her with plenty of entertainment. But use common sense: A nylon bone or two will give her hours of chewing pleasure; a cute plush or rubber toy can be destroyed in two minutes flat, leaving a potentially deadly squeaker in its wake.

Providing water is probably unnecessary in today's temperature-controlled environments. She won't be dehydrating herself with exercise, after all. If you leave water and she drinks it, she'll just have to relieve herself sooner. But she's more likely to entertain herself by spilling it, which means you'll have a mess to clean up when you return—plus, your dog will have spent some time sitting in a wet crate. Again, use common sense.

The first time you crate your hyper dog for more than a few minutes, be sure you have some time to supervise her. If you've provided her with bedding and she seems determined to chew it up, remove it before she has a chance to do any damage. And if she exhibits any other signs of not settling in well—trying to dig her way through the floor, bite her way through the sides, or win your sympathy by yelping in feigned agony—you'll want to be on hand to correct her. Do so by thumping on the crate with your hand the moment she begins misbehaving. Alternatively, leash her and give the leash a jerk; if she's likely to chew on her leash, use a cable instead.

Finally, make it easy on yourself: Teaching her to enter and exit her crate using the In and Out technique described on page 62 will pay off handsomely over time.

How Long Can a Dog Be Crated?

If your dog is sufficiently exercised, and you don't do it regularly, you could *occasionally* crate her for up to eighteen hours. But she must be taken out for potty breaks, exercise, and play for at least 30 minutes after nine of those hours.

This is much longer than most experts would allow. And indeed, it's not a recommendation. But in the real world, it sometimes becomes necessary.

Once your dog is trained, it won't be an issue. She will then be free to move in and out of her crate at will, at least in one room or area of your home.

Beds and Bedding

These days, there's an almost overwhelming choice of dog beds available not only at your local pet supply store, but also online and in mail-order catalogs. What's a loving owner to do?

Among the most important considerations are washability (mandatory), comfort (in particular, cushioning and warmth), and shape (flat, pillow-shaped, or sided). Everything else is just details.

The best place to start is with the realization that, given enough time, a determined or destructive dog can reduce any comfortable bedding to shreds. Sometimes it seems like the more you've paid for a bed, the faster it will fall prey to those sharp teeth. But that's not the biggest problem; far worse is the possibility that your dog will ingest portions of the cover or stuffing and be unable to pass it naturally.

The good news is that most dogs will one day outgrow their chewing. So if you have your heart set on a certain type of bed, chances are you'll eventually be able to make it part of your décor.

Being a bit of a local celebrity, my dog Able (right) has more refined tastes in bedroom furniture, even if his bed *is* tucked away in my walk-in closet. He likes the fact that his wrought-iron bed raises him and his partner, Smartie, up off the floor.

In the meantime, focus your search on bedding made of a tight-ply fabric such as fleece or fake fur. Check the seams: Double or triple stitching is a good sign. Dog trainer Carolyn Sommers, who frequently sews custom bedding for her own dogs and as gifts, recommends upholstery thread plus super-strong French seams, stitched on both sides of the fabric with no raw edges exposed.

You'll find an enormous selection of beds at any large pet supply store. Some dogs seem to prefer those with sides, which provide something to lean on and cuddle up to. Others like to lounge on flat pillow styles. And still others prefer beds that raise them up off the floor a bit.

A foam bed with a removable, washable cover can be very convenient. Keep in mind, however, that on some beds the cover snaps over the foam base like a fitted sheet on a mattress. That means the bottom of the base remains exposed; many an owner has come home to find chunks of foam everywhere, with the cover neatly set aside (or chewed up as well).

Beds with cedar chips are nice from the scent standpoint. Although they zip closed, they present no challenge for a dog bent on destruction.

Polyfill-stuffed cushion beds are a good choice for some dogs. You can even find them tufted these days, to keep the fill from shifting around.

Of course, if you allow your dog up on the couch or even a specific chair, you may not need to bother with a bed at all. Simply cover your furniture with a washable throw—one you've picked up from a local discount store, or a fancy dog-print model from a pet supply catalog, or something in between.

Alternatively, look for another out-of-the-way spot for her to catch naps. When he's not perched on his wrought iron bed, for instance, Able enjoys slipping into the well-blanketed bottom shelf of a built-in cabinet in my condo.

PROBLEM-PROOFING THE ENVIRONMENT

With a little planning and effort, you can keep a wide range of hyper dog misbehaviors from ever becoming an issue in your home.

Puppy- and Dog-Proofing

Some dogs seem to be born with expensive tastes. A Cocker Spaniel of our acquaintance spent his early years chewing up leather belts, leaving nothing but the buckles behind. A Labrador Retriever friend spent his youth devouring textiles, especially throw rugs with tassels and (not surprisingly) pot holders. A Basset Hound boy preferred shoes, purses, wallets, and books, preferably hardcovers fresh from the bookstore. Another Basset loved to munch on her owners' watches and prescription eyeglasses—especially the kind with the $300+ progressive lenses—as well as any exotic plants they decided to try overwintering inside.

Generally speaking, if your hyper dog might find it attractive, you need to keep it out of her reach. Or, if it's something like an overstuffed chair, keep the two apart unless you're around to supervise. That goes for just about anything except for toys you've given to your dog.

You could wait for her to make the objects of her affection known, or you could cross your fingers and hope she's not a chewer. But you'll probably be a happier dog owner if you make an attempt to anticipate her longings and to remove everything that looks like it might be considered a good time by a hyper dog. That includes all the items that the rogue's gallery above focused on, as well as everything from children's toys, knick-knacks, medications, and notepads to small animals, stamps, wicker wastebaskets, and writing instruments.

Not that you'll have to live forever with these items stashed on high shelves and behind closed doors. You just need to wait it out until she's learned to discern between your things and hers, and has gained the level of canine self-control we long for—something that can happen in a matter of months once her first birthday has passed.

Dogs are opportunists. If we leave them alone with a temptation and they simply can't resist, we have no one to blame but ourselves. But cheer up—you're not alone. For proof, visit Caught in the Act at www.dogbreedinfo.com; that's where we discovered chewer extraordinaire Tito of Athens, Greece.

Until that happy day arrives, don't give her any unsupervised freedom in your home. Instead, spy on her constantly or umbilical cord her, equip her with an adequate arsenal of acceptable toys, and consider applying the paste form of Bitter Apple to truly dangerous objects, such as electric cords.

You can also speed the process along with the Shopping technique described on page 69. The goal is to teach her to discriminate between her toys and yours. Toss hers around on the floor and add a generous helping of your own things, including everything from mittens to pens to paperback books. Then leash her and let her browse. Just before she picks up a forbidden item, command "leave it" as you jerk the leash. If your timing is off and she grabs it and refuses to release it with a jerk, spray a little Bitter Apple on her lip line to make her give it up. If she picks up one of her own toys instead, give her high praise.

Repeated often enough, this exercise will teach her to make the right choices consistently—which will, in turn, help transform her into a dog who can be trusted when you're not around to supervise.

Soundproofing

If you're a clever dog owner, your neighbors won't ever hear your home-alone hyper dog raising a ruckus—and your hyper dog won't hear them, either. That's the ideal, anyway, and it's a good goal to shoot for. After all, some neighbors are so intolerant of dogs that they actively look for reasons to complain about yours to landlords, condo associations, or even the police. And some dogs are so distressed by or concerned about neighborhood noises from traffic, construction, or revelry that they can respond destructively in spite of all your careful training.

There are a number of ways to try to keep them from hearing each other, perhaps while providing a continuous sound that your dog will find reassuring. Not sure what will provide comfort, and what will create chaos? You'll simply have to experiment.

Some owners like to leave a radio or television on when they head out the door. That's not a bad idea. Stick around the first few times, though, so you can gauge your dog's reaction from time to time. And since crazy sounds can sometimes emanate from the broadcast media— sounds with the potential to cause more problems than they solve— you might want to try mood CDs or DVDs instead. BowWow TV makes great claims for its Dog-on Television shows, and offers numerous testimonials to back those claims up; check it out at www.bow-wowtv.com, if you're so inclined.

An inexpensive plug-in fountain is a great way to add ambience to your home and simultaneously soothe your dog with the sound of continuously flowing water. Or consider a device that produces low background noise: a fan, air conditioner, clean-air machine, or a device designed specifically to produce white noise.

Still others leave tape recordings of their own voice calmly reading a book, or keep an old-fashioned answering machine hooked up to the phone so they can call home occasionally during the day to say hello to the dog. These are both potentially risky strategies, however, since it can make some dogs anxious when they hear your voice but are unable to find you.

Sometimes it makes sense to confine even a well-trained dog to a room that is removed from potential sources of noise. When he was young and prone to unnecessarily announcing my neighbors' activities, I started barricading Able into the kitchen whenever I left him alone in our condo. My goal was to keep him from hearing, and responding to, every single footstep in the hall outside our door. This strategy seems to have worked, even though our space is quite compact; at least Able has never been the subject of discussion by our condo association's Nuisance Committee—some of whom might have been only too happy to point a finger.

A final thought: Don't throw your windows open on the first warm day of the year, as you're on your way out the door. Instead, wait until you can be home to supervise your dog as she becomes accustomed (or reaccustomed) to the sounds of the neighborhood—and to silence her with the "quiet" command.

Preventing Separation Anxiety

Separation anxiety is as hard on your dog as it can be on your home—and on anyone within hearing distance. That's one good reason for addressing the problem of noise outside your doors. A dog who's already a bit anxious about being left alone can be sent over the edge by sounds she perceives as threatening.

But noise isn't always the culprit. It might be what precedes and follows your absences that sends your dog into a home-alone frenzy—especially if your departures and arrivals are times of high-energy activity and high emotion.

We've already talked about the need for making your own homecomings nonevents by ignoring your dog and her shenanigans for the first fifteen minutes after you arrive. To fight separation anxiety, it's important to do the same thing with your departures. That means ignoring her for fifteen minutes before you leave. Calmly gather your things together so that you don't need to turn into a whirling dervish at the last minute. And then leave without saying a word; don't try to comfort her by explaining your itinerary or giving her an ETA for your return.

> ### Crazy for You?
>
> What exactly happens when you leave home? Does your newly uncrated dog lunge at kids cutting through the yard? Try to get at the mail carrier through the front door? Chase the cat or repeatedly try to jump up on the counters?
>
> There may be clues, such as shredded drapes, scratched cabinets, or plants knocked off the windowsills. If the problem is major, you'll probably want to return to crating; if it's minor, perhaps confining her to a single cozy, safe room with plenty of entertainment will be sufficient.
>
> If you have suspicions but no evidence, you may want to do some sleuthing to determine whether your dog has really earned the privilege of freedom. Or you can try outright spying: I've known owners who have audio- or videotaped their dog during their absences—and discovered some interesting things about how their pooch was spending her time alone.

Some owners trick their dogs into being content during their absences by giving them something especially yummy as they walk out the door—for instance, a Kong toy with a dab of peanut butter hidden inside, or a nylon bone that you've rubbed in your hands so your scent will be on it. It's a great idea—one that can keep a dog happily busy for hours. It can even make your leaving a time for some canine rejoicing.

Others comfort their dog by putting a sweatshirt, nightshirt, or some other recently worn and not washed clothing item on the other side of a closed door. "How far away can he be?" these dogs apparently think. "I'm pretty sure I can smell him in the next room. I'm cool with that."

BOREDOM FIGHTERS

It's true that most dogs will spend a large chunk of their time alone sleeping. It's also true that they can't tell time; you will never see a dog glancing anxiously at the clock, upset that she's been left alone for eight whole hours.

That said, it's also the case that dogs can and do get bored—and a bored canine is too often a destructive canine. Fortunately, hyper dogs are also rather easily amused.

The Toy Chest

If you're like most owners of hyper dogs, you've already invested a small fortune in toys to keep yours happily occupied every waking minute.

If it works, you are indeed fortunate. Self-entertaining dogs who are persistently amused by their toys and never feel the need to look for other outlets for their energy are rare, indeed.

Even if your dog's toy box is already overflowing, you'll no doubt be adding to her collection in the future. Here are a few shopping tips for you.

Dull as they may be, my very favorite toys are hard nylon bones and sterilized bones. They last months, years, and very possibly forever. They take a lot of abuse, absorb a great deal of canine energy, and never leave a mess. Their manufacturers claim that they also clean a dog's teeth; I'm skeptical about that, and suggest regular brushing instead, but this is still my first choice in dog toys.

There are a number of newer chew toys on the market today, many made of virtually indestructible materials such as polyurethane in a variety of inviting shapes and sizes. They're next on my list.

And yet, like any dog owner, I'm attracted to adorable, soft toys. No doubt you'd love to shower your dog with plush teddy bears and cushy dragons, and she would no doubt be delighted. Resist. Unless she has extraordinary powers of discrimination, her experience with them may tempt her to chew on other items made of or covered in soft fabric: clothes, upholstery, her own bedding, even draperies.

Besides, once soft toys are ripped open—something that happens all too easily—they leave a mess and present your dog with tempting stuffing and squeakers. Too often, hyper dogs who start out with one innocent-looking little stuffed toy end up in surgery. If you insist on allowing such toys in your dog's life, be sure to throw them out as soon as she tears the first seam.

Ditto for rope and rawhide toys, which, together with soft toys, have sent many veterinarians' kids through college.

Ingestible items, such as pig ears, cow and horse hooves, cornstarch-based bones, and Greenies, can be good for some dogs. But they're horrible for those with possessive tendencies. Ingestibles seem to bring out the worst in these dogs, and you're asking for trouble if you bring them into your home.

Interactive toys that dispense food when they're rolled around *can* be great; the Buster Cube is a good example. At least one type also enables you to record your voice, rewarding your dog with both audible *and* edible goodies when she nudges it. But such toys are relatively expensive. Since some dogs become easily frustrated with them if the treats aren't ejected quickly enough—or bored with them once they've gobbled up all the treats—give one a try before investing in several.

Probably the very best toys are the unexpected surprises. For instance, I bought my little Obey a Pet Ego Relentless Italian Style dog dish some time ago. She not only eats out of it every day, she also spends a fair chunk of time chewing on the bottom of it. It seems to be indestructible, and she never seems to tire of it.

Other great makeshift toys include empty milk jugs, minus the caps; dogs love to bat them around. Don't leave your dog with one unsupervised, though, in case she manages to bite off a piece.

Windows

Do you want your dog to have a peaceful environment—even if that means not being able to see the world outside your door? Or do you want her to spend her time alone in a mentally stimulating environment, with a full view of everything that's going on in your yard and beyond?

What's right for one dog may not be right for another. You'll probably have to experiment to find out what's best for yours.

In my case, I've usually found a compromise to be the best solution. For example, in my last apartment, I set Obey's crate atop my filing cabinet so she could peer out the window. But she didn't see much more than the occasional bird; her view was limited to a wall of windows across the way. This seemed to be about the right amount of visual stimulation for her. Any more, and she would have barked most of the day.

In fact, dogs who are quietly entertained by watching the outside world are few and far between. Consider limiting your dog's view of the great outdoors to what's visible through a window that is overlooking a tall fence, a hedge, or even another building.

Canine Companions

"I think dogs prefer canine company to any toy imaginable," a woman told me not long ago, "so I have two. When I leave them alone, they're together. I may leave the radio or TV on, but their primary entertainment is each other." She may be right about this for her dogs. But strange as it may seem, it's not always a good idea to leave several dogs together when you're gone.

That's because dogs are pack animals with a well-defined pecking order. And if one dog gets upset for some reason—because someone is ringing the door bell continuously, or because another dog irritates her by encroaching on her space—she may decide to attack.

If you have several dogs, think twice before you leave them alone together, especially for any length of time and especially if there's a large difference in size or age—if one is a puppy or one is elderly, for instance, and the other is an adolescent looking for opportunities to prove himself. Unusual stress could lead to a fight—and possibly, serious injury.

Chapter 7

Tricks of the Trade

Easy, amusing, and amazing tricks for hyper dogs

··

eaching a hyper dog tricks can be a great way to channel his energy into something constructive, to interrupt misbehaviors, and to regain control over him. Unlike straightforward obedience training, tricks offer some truly unique benefits—most notably, they're fun for owner and dog alike, and they can endear our canines to people who are either too hard-hearted or too timid to admire our dogs' exuberance.

In this chapter, I've covered the tricks I've found to be the most popular during the shows my Chihuahua mix, Able, and I put on at events such as the Wisconsin State Fair, as well as many that my students enjoy for their crowd-pleasing and energy-sapping (for the dog) powers.

Your dog may pick them all up immediately. More likely, he'll find a few that he likes and balk at the others. It's no big deal. Feel free to leave a failed trick behind forever.

Or try again later, perhaps when his mood is just right. Able taught me that lesson several years ago, when I was trying to teach him to leap into my arms. He didn't share my enthusiasm for this particular trick. In fact, he flat-out refused to do it, even though I tried endlessly to persuade him that it would be fun.

And then one day a friend came over to visit, and Able was very excited to see him. I squatted to begin demonstrating our newest tricks when, lo and behold, Able leapt into my arms. He accepted additional invitations with increasing enthusiasm. Apparently, he had suddenly decided that it was a fun trick after all—and to this day, it's one of his favorites.

In this case, Able apparently needed to be sufficiently excited to give it a shot. If your dog is stuck, maybe the problem is just that simple. Don't feel that you have to end a trick-training session with a successful performance; if something isn't working, set it aside and try again another day.

THE WAY TO A DOG'S HEART

You'll notice one significant difference in trick training: You use treats (sometimes called "food lures") to get your dog to do what you want him to do.

That's because these are not life-saving commands you're instilling in him. If you find yourself treatless and he refuses to sit up or play dead, it's hardly the end of the world; you can work on it again tomorrow. But if treats are your only way of making sure your dog comes on command and he escapes into the street thirty minutes after gobbling down your last canine cookie, his dependence on food lures could be deadly.

To keep your dog slim and hungry enough to cooperate, use treats cut up so small that they're practically calorie-free; an added benefit is that they'll go down so quickly that the dog won't have to concentrate on chewing. You can buy virtually any brand and type of semi-moist treat and chop it up. You can also use leftover meats such as boneless chicken or hot dogs, diced into pea-sized pieces. Or you can use an economical and nutritious human food, such as Cheerios or veggies.

Instant Hand Signals

It's certainly possible to teach any of the tricks in this chapter without the use of food lures. But treats will make it easier on both of you. A primary reason is that the hand holding the treat can be used to direct the dog's movement. He will quickly recognize this as a hand signal, which is actually far easier for a dog to master than a verbal command.

However, hand signals have the same safety drawbacks as treats: They only work if your dog is totally focused on you, and won't do you much good if your dog is hightailing it in the opposite direction.

> ## Praise Him to the Skies
>
> Don't forget to lavish praise on your dog whenever he per-
> forms a trick properly—and, in the early stages of training,
> even when he gives it a good try. Not only does he deserve it;
> offering your dog abundant, sincere praise increases *your*
> enthusiasm. And that enthusiasm is infectious, making praise
> an extraordinarily beneficial two-way street.

Here's how to use them:

- Before you begin working on a trick, show the dog that you have treats in your hand.

- Use that hand to lure him in the desired directions and positions, holding it tantalizingly close to his nose to keep his interest.

- Try letting him nibble a bit throughout the maneuver; some dogs seem to learn best if they're given a taste of things to come. Experiment to see what works best with your dog.

- Dole out the treats sparingly, and only when he's done what you want him to do.

With this approach, your dog will learn what you want his body to do while achieving the balance and confidence he needs to perform the most popular tricks. If he gets aggressive and tries to get at the treats even when your fingers are in the way, don't assume it was an accident and don't let him get away with it. Give him a bop on the nose with the knuckles of your treat-holding hand.

If, on the other hand, he ignores both you and the treats, it could be that he's not hungry enough. Or maybe you're not holding them close enough to his nose. Or maybe you're moving your hand or your position a little too soon, before he's properly focused; make sure you have his attention before you begin.

ENERGY EATERS

If your hyper dog sometimes seems to enjoy just bouncing off the walls, these tricks are for you. They burn up a great deal of energy in relatively little time. And they seem to delight their performer as much as they do his audience.

- Jumping
- Spinning
- Get your tail
- Weaving
- Circling
- Fancy feet

Jumping

There are several kinds of jumps to try with your dog:

- Leg leaps, such as over your shin, thigh, or calf
- Arm jumps, including over or through the arms

When you've both mastered some of these jumps, you can move on to more complicated maneuvers:

- Patterns, including Around the World
- Anything else you can think of, including leaping into your arms

Getting Started with Leg Leaps

There are three ingredients to teaching the jump: a hungry dog, a leash, and tasty but tiny treats.

Begin by positioning your dog in a sit, parallel to a barrier such as a wall or a couch. Kneel in front of him and create a low jump by extending one leg until it touches the barrier. Hold the treat in the hand farthest from the dog, and show him the treat. When he's focused on it, use the treat to lure him over your leg. When he jumps, praise him and give him the treat.

Treat-Weaning Tips

Once your dog has mastered a trick with treats, begin the process of weaning him off the treats. Set him up for a trick the same way you always did, holding and moving your hand as if it were holding a lure—but leaving the food in your pocket for now.

Say "good dog" when he looks at your hand. Then give him the appropriate command and lure him through the maneuver with your still-empty hand. Repeat this a time or two before reaching into your pocket for his treat. If he refuses, use the collar and leash to manipulate him through the maneuver and praise him enthusiastically when he complies— even if you're actually doing the hard work.

You don't need to phase the food out entirely. You may still want to use treats to fire up his enthusiasm during warm-ups or if he seems to be going stale on a trick you repeat frequently. Consider using them to phase new tricks into your repertoire. And whenever you drop something edible on the floor, don't waste it; let your dog have it *after* he's done a trick for you.

Then reverse the process, luring him back over your leg with the other hand. You may need to put the hand without the treat behind your back or neck so he won't be distracted by it (since it was, after all, the source of the preceding treat).

Once he's following the lure reliably, add a command such as "over" a split second before luring him. When he begins responding to this command, you can start weaning him off the treats (see the box on this page for tips on how to do that).

Here are a few success-building tips:

- Try to anticipate when your dog is likely to go off course. Use the food lures or leash to keep him on track.

- Don't jerk the leash. Instead, pull it—and praise him lavishly when he responds properly.

- Keep the jumps low until he's responding to the "over" command. Then raise them gradually to build his confidence bit by bit.

Take It a Step at a Time

Put some treats in each hand and position your dog in a sit parallel to a barrier. Form a low jump with your leg. Now, show the dog the treat in your far hand.

Use the treat to lure him over your leg. Eventually, your hand movement will become his cue for jumping over your leg even when there are no treats.

You envision a trick as a whole. But in fairness to your dog, remember that it's actually a series of smaller tasks. He'll learn far more quickly if you "deconstruct" each trick, breaking it down into its basic components and then building his confidence every step of the way. As his concentration improves, delay the reward until he has completed two steps, then three, and eventually the entire trick.

Consider how you might apply this step-by-step approach to creating a choreographed series of leg and arm leaps, using the techniques outlined in this section on jumping.

The first step is achieving a very low leg jump, with your foot against a barrier so your dog has no option except to step over it. Reward him for his success by giving him a treat. Once he's mastered this low hurdle, raise your leg in two- or three-inch increments until he's actually leaping over it.

Then repeat the process, this time directing him over your calf . . . and then over an arm. Again, maintain the barrier but raise the height of the jump incrementally.

Next, go back to the beginning and repeat the entire process—this time without the barrier.

Once he's mastered these component jumps, take your show on the road, practicing in new locations and in the presence of increasingly tempting distractions. (Keep a line on him to maintain control.)

Now you can start mixing it up, combining various leg and arm leaps into a mini canine ballet.

When it comes to deconstructing tricks, there are no hard and fast rules. Consider this approach to be a guideline; develop your own techniques if you prefer, referring back to these suggestions if you're not making satisfactory progress.

If your dog is long-bodied and can reach your hand without going over your leg, toss the treat in the direction you want him to go.

He'll have to jump over to get it.

Leg Leap Variations

. . . the over-the-thigh Grand Plie . . .

Variations on the leg leap include the standing, over-the-shin CanCan . . .

. . . the over-the-calf Flapper . . .

. . . and the Hip-Hop, in which the dog leaps through your angled leg.

You may need a helper (and perhaps a leash) to teach some of these jumps, especially the Hip-Hop.

Your helper uses the lure and the leash to help the dog understand what you want him to do.

Arm Jumps

Follow the same basic steps for arm jumps that you used to teach your dog leg leaps. Begin by putting him in a sit parallel to a barrier, kneeling in front of him, and extending your arm to create a low jump. Once he's

The basic High Jump over-arm leap is simplest. You can place something narrow under your out-stretched arm to block off the under-arm route—a small suitcase, for instance.

Then toss the treat over your shoulder and your dog will follow.

Once you have this basic technique down, you can use your arms to create a variety of hoop-type jumps. Your imagination is your only limitation. I call this sidearm version the Hole in One.

This is Shot Put. You wouldn't want to try it with a Great Dane.

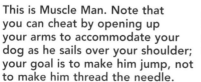

This is Muscle Man. Note that you can cheat by opening up your arms to accommodate your dog as he sails over your shoulder; your goal is to make him jump, not to make him thread the needle.

Jumping sticks and hula hoops are fun and theatrical, and an easy (if slightly less convenient) variation on arm and leg jumps.

got these not-very-high jumps down pat, you can gradually raise the bar by crouching or standing bent at the waist—it depends on the size, build, and athleticism of your dog. Then you can begin creating unusual jumps such as those shown in the photos on this page and page 128.

Since arm jumps are more difficult to teach than leg leaps, plan on tossing the treats. Better yet, grab a leash and a helper to make it clear to your dog what you want him to do by having the helper jump with the dog, using the leash to guide him. The learning curve will be shorter for both of you, and you and your helper will have fun turning your hyper dog into a star performer.

Patterns

Here's where jumping gets really exciting. All you're doing is combining various leg and arm jumps, but the result can be pretty spectacular. Pick your favorites, combine them, and you'll have your own act to wow your friends and family.

Your dog will obviously have to be proficient with the component jumps before moving on to this level.

Any jumping pattern that brings your dog back to his original starting point is called Around the World. This one combines the Flapper calf jump with the Hole in One.

I call this Around the World pattern the M jump. Not pictured are Able's landings and pivots between leaps.

Note that my head indicates the direction he is to travel—a cue a dog picks up on through repetition.

The Merry-Go-Round involves leaping up over the thigh . . .

. . . circling back to jump the calf . . .

. . . and coming back around over the thigh once again.

And the Rest

It gets even more interesting! Once your hyper dog has mastered a series of basic leg and arm jumps and some patterns, you can teach star-quality jumps such as leaping into your arms—a trick best suited for small and medium dogs.

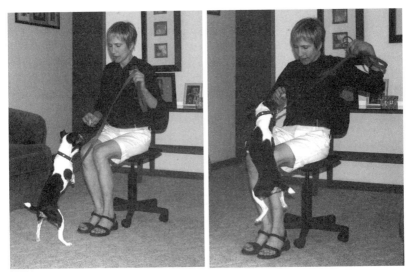

To teach your dog to leap in your arms, grab some treats, have a seat, and . . .

. . . lure him up into your lap.

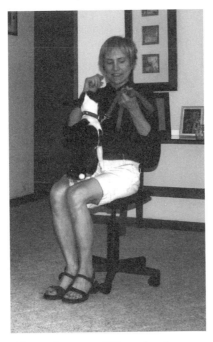

After a few repetitions, begin adding a command such as "hup" when you want him to jump.

Choose Your Cues Carefully

The commands I've used here are only idea-starters. Use whatever words, cues, and hand signals you want. You could even use foreign words to make your dog appear to be multilingual. Or you can train without words, relying exclusively on body cues and hand signals.

If you decide to use commands, try to group them according to the physical demands they'll place on your dog.

"Jump" or "over," for example, instructs the dog to jump over something. It implies that he'll end up back where he started—on the floor or ground.

"Up" or "hup," on the other hand, tells him to jump up and land on something at a higher level—perhaps your lap.

To you, it may look like he's doing the same thing in each case, but the physical requirements are actually quite different for him; using a different word can help him launch himself appropriately.

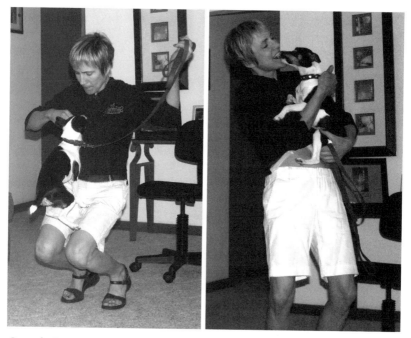

Once he's an expert at this seated leap, stand up slightly and repeat the process. Bend your legs, not your back; you don't want to be hulking over him when he leaps.

Continue standing up a little more for each leap. When you've reached a full stand, lean back just a bit so he'll have a sort of landing pad. You can add a chest pat to the "hup."

Leaping onto Your Back

You'll want a partner to help you teach this trick. It may be possible to do it without assistance, but you have to manipulate your body like a contortionist to do so.

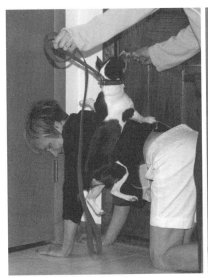 

Get down on your hands and knees and have your helper position your leashed dog at your side, a short leap away. Ask your helper to lure him onto your back with a treat. After a few repetitions, tell your dog "hup" as the helper is luring him. When he's aboard your back, have your helper give him both a treat and lavish praise.

If one trick isn't enough for you, add "sit up" to the scenario. Then use a bright "okay" or "off" to release him.

Finally, use the leash . . .

. . . and treats to lure your dog onto your back solo.

Jumping onto my back is probably Able's favorite trick—especially when he's in the middle of a performance.

Spinning

Some dogs naturally love to spin, often favoring one direction over the other. Others need some prompting. Either way, here's how to turn this form of canine dancing on and off.

Hold Off on that Cue

With tricks, it's generally a good idea to delay adding a verbal cue until you're both able to do the trick easily using food lures and hand motions. You're both learning to coordinate relatively complex motions, balance, and weight shifts, essentially building muscle memory with the goal of one day executing each trick almost effortlessly.

If you add a command too early in the learning process, while your dog is still is confused and is therefore trying every variation, the parameters of the command will not be clear to him; it will take him longer to learn its precise meaning. So make your mistakes in the absence of commands, adding words only when both of you have become proficient.

Begin teaching the spin in a corner to limit your dog's working area.

Lure him around in a tight circle. At first, reward him with treats and praise for even a partial turn. Expect a full turn after about a dozen attempts.

After a few sessions, begin weaning him off the food, using hand signals and a leash, if necessary, to get him started. Then add a command: I use an ironic "relax" for clockwise turns, "chill" for counterclockwise.

With a larger dog, keep your hand low so that he will twist his body around to get the treat.

Spinning Variations

Once your dog has the basic spin moves down, it may become his favorite thing to do—especially when he's uncertain about what you want from him. Take this as a sign that he'd enjoy learning to elaborate on the basic spin. Have him switch directions to music, for instance, or invite him to move backward or forward while spinning or to spin alongside you as you walk.

Unable to contain their enthusiasm for spinning, small dogs will quite naturally want to play helicopter, spinning in midair.

Get Your Tail

Some dogs have a proclivity for chasing their tails. You can encourage it, if you like, with an enthusiastic "good good good" and "chase your tail" when you see your dog doing it.

If he has never shown any interest in this activity but you'd like him to give it a try, you can put some peanut butter or honey on his tail.

Some dogs won't ever have any interest in tail-chasing. Since it has been known to become a compulsion in certain dogs, don't push it; there are plenty of other fun tricks to work on.

Weaving

Imagine walking along with your dog zigzagging back and forth between your legs, without a misstep on your part or his. That's what weaving looks like once you two have mastered it—and it's a pretty impressive looking piece of footwork!

When your dog takes interest in the treat, use it to lure him through your legs.

When he succeeds, give him both treat and praise.

Take a giant step forward and reverse the process.

All you need are some food lures. Begin by putting your dog in a sit-stay, then showing him the treat in your hand. Move a step or two away from him and take a giant step forward with the leg farthest from him. Show him the treat in your farther hand, positioned between your legs, and say, "Okay, good buddy!" Then follow the steps shown in the photos on this page.

Continue taking steps forward and drawing him through. Then add the "weave" command.

Within a few sessions, he should respond to the command without the need for the lures, and you'll be able to step up your pace to a slow walk.

Swaying Weave

This simple variation enables you to stay put while your dog does all the work. Once you've learned the basic weave, it'll be a piece of cake. With a little practice, you should be able to sway back and forth from leg to leg with your dog dashing through the shifting opening created by your legs.

To teach the swaying weave, step to the side with a slight bend in your leg, display the food lure enticingly, and command "weave." Once the dog has gone through your legs, lure him back around to the front. Then repeat on the other side, shifting your weight to the opposite leg. You'll eventually be able to do this quickly and smoothly.

Grapevine Weave

If you've ever taken step aerobics, you're already familiar with the grapevine pattern. If not, it's a simple but smooth sidestepping pattern, usually done by crossing one foot behind the other. Once your dog has the basic weave down, you can easily add this maneuver to your repertoire. Here's how.

Put your dog in a sit-stay and have treats in both your hands. Show him a treat, step away from him, and stand facing him with your feet three feet apart. Say, "Okay buddy, weave." Use the lure in your right hand to bring him through your legs and back around your right leg to his original position.

Take a grapevine step to your left and repeat the process . . . again and again and again. Soon, you'll be working in one continuous flow.

Circling

To teach your hyper dog to circle objects or people, start out with something like a tall wastebasket—something big enough in diameter so the dog will recognize it as a solid object, and short enough that you can sweep your arm over it.

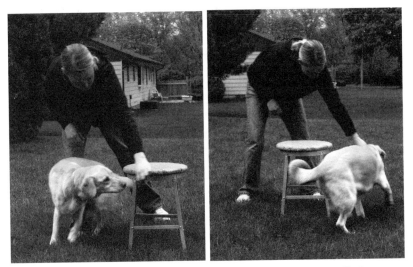

Use a treat to lure your dog around the object.

This motion will eventually become a hand signal.

Begin by luring him around the object with a treat. After a few successes, introduce a command; I use "pole" for a clockwise circle, "loop" for counterclockwise. Use whatever words work for you—or skip the words and just use hand signals.

Once he's got this down, you can trade the object for a person. Follow the same procedure: lure if necessary, and add commands if you like. I use "circle" for a clockwise turn around a person, "wee" for counterclockwise.

When he's mastered both kinds of circling, you can combine them, much to an observer's amusement. Try figure-8s, for instance, using the "circle" and "loop" commands in conjunction with a friend or assistant and a handy object.

Fancy Feet

You can combine any of the tricks I've already described into a series of exciting and energy-draining feats. It's great for your dog's amusement and yours, for entertaining company, and for pre-empting bad behavior when you see trouble on the horizon—for instance, if you're out walking him and spot a dog he doesn't like rounding the corner. It's actually very much like the Rapid-fire Commands described in chapter 10, but more interesting.

Combine these tricks any way you please, incorporating some basic obedience drills, too. For instance:

- Spin, spin, down, spin, spin, down
- Spin, heel, weave, loop, jump
- Jump, jump, weave, sit
- Grapevine weave, sit, you step back, he jumps into your arms

CONTROL GRABBERS

When you want to cleverly demonstrate control without any of the outpouring of activity involved in our energy eaters, one or more of these tricks might be just what you need. They may not burn up as much energy, but they require concentration and obedience—two things that can turn a hyper dog into the epitome of good behavior.

- Magic marker
- Balancing treats
- Sitting up
- Dead dog

Magic Marker

This is a great trick whenever you want to keep your dog out of a particular area—if you're playing a board game on the floor, for instance, or want him to stay a certain distance from the picnic table.

Simply use an object such as a leash, belt, tie, or even a roll of wrapping paper to "magically" mark a line that he is not to cross. You convey this concept by waiting until he does try to cross the line and then issuing the "wait" command. If he continues forward, elbow him back

You can turn a plain old leash into an instant fence with the Magic Marker technique.

and praise him. When you're finished, pick up your Magic Marker and release him with the "chin-touch okay." Repeat as needed, eventually eliminating the commands entirely.

When you're ready to use this trick for real, simply place the marker and watch everyone eyeing your dog in amazement as he refuses to cross it. When you're finished, pick up your magic marker and watch for more raised eyebrows as he scampers happily into the once-forbidden territory.

Balancing Treats

We've all seen adorable dogs balancing a biscuit on their noses—at least on television. It's a striking demonstration of self-control. And it's one that is especially useful when visitors have just arrived; it's tough to balance a treat while you're jumping up on people!

What's more, this trick is not difficult to teach. Begin by putting your dog into a sit-stay. Put a treat on his nose and hold his face, saying "easy . . . easy . . . easy" in a soothing tone of voice. Then say "okay" as you remove your hands and allow him to wolf down the treat.

Put your dog into a sit-stay. Put a treat on his nose and hold his face, saying "easy . . . easy . . . easy."

Say "okay" as you remove your hands and let him catch the treat.

Repeat this process, reducing the "easies" as well as your hand pressure. Gradually increase the time between removing your hands and saying "okay." Eventually, step away from him, saying "okay" at your discretion.

Sitting Up

Here's another charming, old-fashioned trick that's great to save for when company arrives, or any other time you want to distract your dog from his activity of choice. It's no tougher than the balancing trick just described, but instead of self-control, it requires good balance.

Start out by putting your dog in a straight sit against a wall. Don't let him lean on one haunch or the other. The wall will keep him from backing away and will provide him with a little help in the balance department when he's just starting out.

Begin by holding your dog by the collar so he can't move away, and bring the lure close to his nose. Raise your hand slowly, adjusting the distance from your body to help him find his natural balance point. The idea is to get him to come up for the treat without losing his "sit."

Some dogs are naturals, finding their balance point almost instantly. Others need a lot of repetition. And some will always look like a slight breeze would knock them over. But even clumsiness can be endearing in a hyper dog who is trying his best to do a trick for you.

A sit-up can be calming, because the dog must really focus to maintain the position—and it adds a lot of cuteness points to the equation. You can use it everywhere, from the vet's office to at home around guests.

Dead Dog

This is a great trick for kids. It's also a good way to promote compliance during everything from nail trimming and tooth brushing to bandaging a paw and checking for fleas.

To get started, put your dog into a "down" and roll him onto his side. Place your hand on his head to get him to rest it on the floor and calmly say "dead dog." Praise him gently.

Every time he tries to raise his head, push him back down gently but firmly and soothingly say, "good." Gradually back away from him, returning occasionally to give him a soothing stroke or to push his head back down.

When you're finished, return to him and use the "chin-touch okay" to release him.

With your dog lying on his side, head on the ground, gradually back away. If he tries to raise his head, push it back down while saying "good" in a soothing tone of voice.

A Little Help from Your Friends

Sometimes your hyper dog is not the most popular canine among the people you care about. But you'll find folks warming up to him when he does tricks for them—especially if you invite them to participate.

The jumps are probably the easiest to practice with a willing helper. If they can put out a leg or hold a jumping stick or hula hoop, you can do the commanding and luring. Sitting up for a treat is easy, too—your friend won't have to say a word.

If you've platform-trained your dog and you sense that this person would rather your dog stayed away, you can invite him or her to tell your dog to go to his platform. That way, your friend gets rid of the dog without feeling rude, and feels empowered by giving the command.

Of course, your dog probably won't obey. Calmly enforce the command even though he isn't being disobedient deliberately; when other people give a discriminating dog a command, he'll ignore it because they're not authority figures to him.

If you want him to obey a particular person, work with them both—definitely something you'll need to do with other members of your household, or with someone who will be caring for your dog while you're out of town.

CLICKER TRAINING

A clicker is a nifty little noisemaker that enables you to teach your hyper dog even complex commands very quickly—in some cases, commands for actions that couldn't be taught any other way. It also lets you deliver feedback to your dog without emotion, so that you can't personally distract him from learning.

This technique is not quite an exact science, and there are probably as many clicker-training techniques as there are clicker trainers. There are also a growing number of articles and books on the subject. Want to learn more than we can cover in this section? Gary Wilkes' web site at www.clickandtreat.com is a great place to begin.

The idea behind clicker training is to condition a dog to perform a very specific behavior to earn a food treat. Whether the arrival of this treat is immediate or delayed, it's always used in conjunction with a well-timed click that will come to mean "Great job, buddy—what you did at this particular nanosecond was just what I wanted!" Eventually, you add a command or a physical signal to each desired action, so that the dog can distinguish between the various "clickered" activities.

The sky's the limit to what you can teach your dog using a clicker. I personally don't recommend using it for ordinary obedience commands, such as those discussed in chapter 3. Although it certainly can be used for those commands, it's comparatively convoluted and time-consuming and, in my experience, potentially unreliable.

But for more complex tricks and even some nearly-impossible-to-teach activities, arm yourself with a clicker and a bit of diced chicken, and you'll be ready to roll. Here are a couple of examples.

Clicker Curtsy

Bowing—or curtsying, as we're going to call it, to avoid confusing your dog with a word that sounds too much like "down"—is ordinarily a difficult command to teach. Dogs do it naturally when they're stretching or playing, but only for a split second.

Your dog's first attempts at the curtsy may look a little strange, but keep at it. Click just before his elbows hit the ground.

That's where a precisely timed click comes into play as positive reinforcement. Try it yourself. Here's how.

Hang out with your dog, clicker and treats at the ready, until he naturally assumes the "curtsy" position. Click instantly and give him a treat.

If he's not buying it, use a treat to manipulate him into position. Click the moment he does it, and again, give him a treat. Do it again and again, until you've given him half a dozen treats. Do three sessions a day, if you have time. When he seems to be getting it, command "curtsy" just before his elbows hit the ground. Click and treat as usual. Keep using the command "curtsy," and extend the time between click and treat until the click has become his reward.

Laser Chase

This is a fun way to pass a rainy night indoors . . . or a starlit night outside.

It's a good idea to prepare for this trick in advance, placing treats around various spots in your home. Make a mental note of where you've left them, so you'll be able to find them before your dog does.

Then take him near the first treat and use a flashlight or a laser pointer to point it out. Tell him "okay" or "get it" or something similar to give him permission to pounce on the treat, and click just before he gobbles it down. Then use the laser light to trace the path to the next treat and the next, each time clicking just before he grabs the treat. Your goal is to get him to follow the light and to think of the click and the treat as one reward. When he becomes interested in following the laser, wean him off the treats and the clicker.

Once your dog begins following the laser reliably at night, you'll be ready to perform this trick in the light of day.

Use the light to point out each treat, and click when the dog is about to devour it. Eventually you'll wean him from the treats and the clicker so that he's simply chasing the light.

Clicker Skateboarding

Picture a dog skateboarding. Now picture *your* dog skateboarding!

Believe it or not, this scenario *is* achievable. Clicker training is what makes it possible even for dog-and-owner duos who aren't in training for Hollywood roles. Here's the process.

Get your dog accustomed to riding around on wheels. Lure him into a cart, give him a treat, and praise him. Repeat this several times. Then take him on a slow ride, holding his collar to prevent him from jumping ship, and give him treats and praise as you go.

In the meantime, build yourself an instant doggie teeter-totter out of a 4x4-foot board. Take four strips of wood and nail them to the bottom of the board in a square that is just large enough to accommodate a tennis ball. Turn the contraption over and set the square over a ball. You have just created a device to get your dog used to riding on an unstable surface.

Help him do so by leading him onto and over the board over and over again. Use treats to lure him if necessary. It may take a while for him to get used to the tipping, but it's a necessary foundation for skateboarding.

Temporarily stabilize the skateboard before you first ask your dog to climb aboard.

When climbing aboard a skateboard has become a non-event for him, give the skateboard a little push. Gradually build up distance and speed.

Once he's comfortable with it, substitute a skateboard, temporarily making it stationary with blocks. Use treats to lure him aboard if necessary.

Eventually, standing aboard a skateboard will become second nature to him. At that point, remove the blocks and give the board a little push. Gradually increase the length of his ride and his speed.

Chapter 8

Organized Sports

Sensational solutions for team players

···

We're social creatures, we humans. So are our dogs. And that may be the primary reason so many of us gravitate toward organized canine sports. They are a phenomenal way to meet people who share our passion for our hyper dogs and our interest in particular activities.

But that's hardly the only reason for investigating organized sports. Consider variety. You can only go through the heel, sit, down, stay, and come routine so often before new challenges start looking mighty good—especially for a dog who's hyperactive both mentally and physically. Organized sports can be a great way to inject variety into her routine while you both pick up new skills.

Then there's the desire to outdo our peers. Some people and dogs are inherently competitive, and organized sports can be the only way they feel they can really shine.

For some of us, organized sports can provide motivation that might otherwise be lacking. We're more likely to leave behind the office or kitchen or television room and to practice with our dogs if our efforts will soon be subject to public scrutiny. And we're more likely to step beyond the boundaries of our own yard or neighborhood if other people and dogs are waiting for us.

For some of us, organized sports also offer us a great bonding experience and—strange as it may sound to most people—a way to make our hyper dogs *very* happy. "My dog doesn't need to be exhausted to be content," says Amiable instructor Barb Pierce, owner of a young Border Collie named Dottie. "But she does need to be stimulated mentally. Otherwise, she'll be bored."

To preclude that possibility, Barb trains her dog in both obedience and agility. She's somewhat of an old hand at it; Dottie is the third dog

151

she has taken through such a training regimen. They've all enjoyed it, she says—as has she, thanks to her dogs' hyper energy and personalities.

THE RIGHT SPORT FOR YOU

Whatever your interests, energy level, and budget, you'll find an organized canine sport to fit them. It doesn't matter if your dog is a purebred of impeccable lineage or a mixed breed whose family tree has been forever lost to history: If you've got control over her, there are people and hyper dogs out there waiting to welcome you into their fold.

Energy Level

Most of the sports covered in this chapter share two important traits: They're all great energy burners for hyper dogs, and they are not especially demanding of *your* energy.

Agility training is the most notable exception, since handlers run the course with their dogs. But there are exceptions here, too. I know one older man who has such great control over his dogs that he barely moves, relying primarily on hand and voice cues to direct them. For him, agility doesn't present any insurmountable physical challenges.

Your Personal Interests

It makes sense to choose a sport based on your personal interests. If none of those discussed in this chapter appeal to you, use your imagination and a good Internet search engine, and you'll probably come up with exactly the right activity for you.

In fact, you'll find a great deal of information on every possible permutation of organized canine sports on the Internet. The American Kennel Club's web site (www.akc.org) is a good place to begin; select "Clubs" on the AKC's home page and explore to your heart's content. The United Kennel Club (www.ukcdogs.com) is another good place to check out, especially if your hyper dog is a mixed breed. Another favorite site of mine is www.dogplay.com, which covers both dog sports and organizations to help you get started.

Your Dog's Aptitude

Is your dog a scenthound or sighthound? Does she have a powerful chase instinct? Does she love the water, or digging, or pulling?

Sometimes such traits can point you in the right direction. A dog who loves to swim might be perfect for dock diving, for example, while a sheepdog might be more sensibly steered in the direction of organized herding. Take some time to learn about the purposes for which your dog's breed (or combination of breeds) was developed, and see if this might suggest the best course for her.

But don't rely solely on canine preferences or breed to dictate your choice of organized sport. Like children, dogs can lose interest in an activity as soon as it becomes mandatory. A Husky who pulls you down the street may be a complete bust as a sled dog. An Airedale who ordinarily spends her life with her nose to the ground could turn out to be an unenthusiastic tracking dog.

Nor can we stereotype dogs based on breed alone; individual animals can really surprise us. For instance, one herding enthusiast I know raves about a Springer Spaniel who became an adept and enthusiastic herding dog. And Doug Kennedy, who conducts hunting dog classes at his kennel, Water Dog Specialties, reports that his students occasionally include Poodles and Portuguese Water Dogs.

Bottom line: Given the proper guidance and an environment of contagious enthusiasm, a dog's abilities may far surpass our initial expectations. Besides, it can be a lot of fun having a novel breed in a sport and winning the "underdog" vote from your peers.

Expense

The cost of participating in organized sports can vary a great deal. And, like just about any other competitive sport, it can be quite expensive.

For instance, if your training skills are average or below and you're not great at translating the information in books or articles to the real world of dog training, you'll probably want to get some type of instruction. Group instruction is obviously less expensive than private lessons, and offers the added advantage of enabling you and your dog to practice around often extreme distractions. Or you may luck out and find a group of people who get together for the sheer joy of teaching each other, without any fee; this is quite common in tracking, for instance.

In some cases—and this is especially common in field trials and hunt tests—you may decide to hire a professional trainer for your dog, which can translate into a heavy tab.

In other cases, you'll have to make an upfront investment in equipment. That's the case with carting, sledding, and weight pulling, for instance. And, like anything else, you can spend as much as you want. Brand new premium equipment can be expensive; used low-end equipment can sometimes be had for a song.

Entry fees and travel expenses can also add up. And you should know that these costs are rarely covered by prize money or stud fees. Still, this fact seldom deters enthusiasts—not even those of very modest means. Which may confirm that bonding with one's dog is a priceless experience.

The Only Real Prerequisite

In most cases, no one will expect you or your dog to walk in, ready to roll. And while there will always be rude and haughty people in just about any group, you're sure to find some extremely knowledgeable, kind, and eager souls to help you both learn the ropes.

That said, do be sure you have solid control over your dog before you attempt to participate in any organized activity. You won't be invited back if she lunges and snaps at other dogs or howls nonstop from the moment you arrive, or is in any other way disruptive. And if this is the right sport for you, you'll definitely want to be invited back.

The good news is that some sports involve practically no cost. For Frisbee groups, for instance, you just need a disk and a dog. For herding, if you've already got livestock, you don't even need the disk! And for agility, although you could invest in the costly course equipment yourself, you don't have to; you can simply train in classes, enjoying the companionship of like-mined enthusiasts and the added benefit of ready distractions for your dog.

Time Commitment

Although some organized canine activities require a considerable time investment for training, you may be able to do much of the foundation work solo. That means you'll be able to squeeze in ten minutes here or there at your convenience, before work or as part of your daily outings. Examples include Frisbee, freestyle dancing, and obedience.

Others will require anywhere from a couple of hours regularly to full days. These time-hungry sports include hunting, tracking, lure coursing, earthdog, and dock diving.

Cleanliness

Unfortunately, there aren't too many organized canine sports that enable you to duck out on your lunch hour, train your dog, and return to work without cleaning up. If you don't like getting dirty, or don't have time to do so, you'll want to stick with activities such as obedience, rally-O, and freestyle.

The rest are not for neat freaks. Hunting, tracking, and herding can be a bit messy. You can work up a real sweat with agility. Any time you use ropes (also known as lines) with dogs—as in the case with carting and sledding—you're going to get dirty. Even that innocent-looking little Frisbee will leave your hands in need of a good lathering. And if your dog froths at the mouth when she exerts herself, you'll probably be wearing a few tell-tale signs when you're finished practicing any sport.

Breed

Some activities, such as earthdog tests and lure coursing, may be open only to certain breeds. Some require that your dog be purebred and registered with the event's governing body, such as the AKC. Most events are also open to dogs who've been granted only limited registration or an indefinite listing privilege (ILP). And some run fun competitions for dogs of any breed. So if you find one door closed because your dog is a Heinz 57, don't assume she'll have to be a benchwarmer.

AGILITY

If you've ever watched a well-trained dog negotiate a complex obstacle course, completely tuned in to her owner's precisely timed movements and directions, you'll begin to understand why some owners and their dogs find this sport so compelling. The obstacles range from teeter-totters and weave poles to jumps, A-frames, and tunnels, and the velocity ranges from break-neck speed to trotting to pausing.

A Border Collie carefully negotiates the contact point on an agility teeter-totter.

Despite the fact that Missie Peterman initially brought Miss Melonie to class simply to gain some control over her, they ultimately discovered a shared passion in agility. In fact, Miss Melonie ended up becoming the first American Pit Bull Terrier to earn a Grand Agility Championship title.

Agility trials are held by a range of organizations, including the North American Dog Agility Council, United States Dog Agility Association, UKC, and AKC. They're tailored to dogs of virtually any breed, size, and skill level, too—including novice. Classes to train owners and dogs are widely available.

Be forewarned: Chances are good that you'll both find this sport so exciting that it becomes addictive. In fact, despite the initial expense, maintenance, and space requirements, many agility students buy key obstacles so they can practice at home between classes and competitions.

Jody Yehle, an instructor at Amiable Dog Training, reports that agility has been ideal for Conner, her hyper young Border Collie-Heeler mix. "Just walking or running with him isn't enough," she says. "Not even obedience is quite enough. If he doesn't go to agility class every week, he's very unhappy. When he *does* go, he's less edgy and more attentive to me, and he leaves the cats alone."

Missie Peterman agrees, pointing out that agility does more than just keep a dog in great shape. "Your dog needs to have full attention on you to be able to follow your directions with split-second timing," says this owner-handler, whose American Pit Bull Terrier, Miss Melonie, was the first of this breed to earn a Grand Agility Championship title (U-GRACH). "It's a great sport for keeping your dog both physically and mentally fit."

CANINE FREESTYLE

Has your hyper dog got a little rhythm? Have you? Then consider canine freestyle, which seamlessly merges the commands you've taught her with music and movement.

Other than a solid grasp of the basic commands outlined in chapter 3, you don't need any special training to put on quite a show. Simply choose a piece of music, two to three minutes long, that you can walk in time to. Make sure that it's something you're fairly crazy about, because you'll be listening to it over and over again.

Some canine freestylers opt for classical music. It's especially fun to watch a performance using instruments that reflect the dog's size or character—for instance, music prominently featuring a piccolo for a jaunty little dog such as a Yorkie Poo or Min Pin, or a bassoon-heavy symphony for a Clumber Spaniel or Rottweiler. Or you can choose something more contemporary—maybe some Motown, rock, soul, or country-western.

Once you've chosen the music, create a routine to go with it. Use your repertoire of obedience and trick commands, expecting that there will be quite a bit of improvisation taking place as your performance develops. Say, for instance, you've chosen a three-minute section of Prokofiev's *Peter and the Wolf.* You might create a routine in which you glide along through a series of figure-8s while your dog heels, spins, and jumps at your side.

It's generally easiest to create, develop, and properly execute a routine if you break it down into sections containing, at most, two or three moves. Practice each thoroughly, then link the sections together, and you'll be ready to perform.

There are currently three freestyle organizations to help you get started. Check these web sites for listings of upcoming events and demonstrations, training tips, tapes on training and actual competitions, and for a peek at some of the coolest freestyle routines imaginable.

- World Canine Freestyle Organization, www.worldcanine-freestyle.org
- Canine Freestyle Federation, www.canine-freestyle.org
- Musical Dog Sport Association, www.musicaldogsport.org

You don't have to become active in any of these organizations, of course. And in fact, you may never take your show on the road, preferring to perform it audience-free for life. Or you might want to build up an entire repertoire and take your performance to entertain people at a nursing home or a children's hospital—just two spots where you're bound to find appreciative and enthusiastic audiences.

Either way, I think I can promise that a good time will be had by all—even if that just means you and your hyper dog.

Able the Dancing Dog and Amy are regulars on the Children's Stage at the Wisconsin State Fair and other family-friendly festivals. In between routines, we educate kids about dog safety and how to be a dog's best friend.

CANINE FRISBEE

Another fine product of the late 1960s and early 1970s, canine Frisbee can be played alone with your hyper dog, in clubs, and competitively.

You won't find a sport with a much lower cost of entry: All it takes is a few bucks for the plastic disc. And for the retrieve-happy hound, it doesn't take a lot of training to get started. If she doesn't go for the flying disc naturally, you can train her to respond to the "catch" command by tossing food her way at first . . . and later a tennis ball.

Once she has the catch down, add the retrieving component, and encourage her to jump toward and grab a disk held just above her eye-level.

In fact, the toughest part of playing canine Frisbee may be you learning to throw the disc properly.

CARTING, DRAFTING, AND SLEDDING

As long as your hyper dog has some size—fifty pounds or over, although this is not a hard and fast rule—and vet-confirmed good health, you can add harness-drawn activities such as carting, drafting, and sledding to your list of energy-eating alternatives.

The principles are pretty much the same for all these activities. In fact, the big difference between carting and drafting is that drafting implies hauling work loads. Only the weather, equipment, and accessories vary.

Before you begin, familiarize yourself with these sports by browsing online and checking out some books, magazines, and videos on the subject; there are plenty available on sledding, in particular. For instance, *Mushing* magazine and books such as *Mush* and *Training the Lead Dog* offer a wealth of information for the novice. Another useful book, highly recommended by Newfoundland enthusiast Bonnie Kaufman, is *Newfoundland Draft Work* by Consie Power. And check out web sites such as www.dogworks.com and www.mrcrottweiler.org for further insights into these disciplines.

If your initial investigations leave you feeling intrigued, find a local club so you can meet some of the people you'll be hanging out with and see what sort of upfront assistance will be available. Among the best resources we've found for this is www.sleddogcentral.com, which includes links to nearby clubs.

Are all systems still go? Then it's time to start outfitting your dog.

The most important piece of equipment you'll need is a properly fitting harness. You'll find an endless variety available from outfitters online, along with measuring instructions; it definitely pays to measure carefully. You'll also want to start looking for the rest of your equipment—most notably, a sled or cart, or both. You can spend hundreds on each, or search for used equipment in your local newspaper, on the Internet, or from your new friends at the club.

In the meantime, you can get started on teaching your dog some new commands that will enable you to control her

Reva Reinelt and her team of Alaskan Malamutes enjoy the serenity of a wintry Wisconsin trail.

from behind. The first is to move forward even though you're not at her side. Use a word or phrase such as "hike" or "let's go" or "all right."

Second, she'll have to know when you want her to go right or left. The traditional words are "gee" for right and "haw" for left. Third, she'll have to know when to slow down and to stop. Here, horseback-riding commands are useful: "easy" for slow down and "whoa" for stop.

The simplest way to teach these commands is to use your new vocabulary as opportunities arise—for instance, when walking or biking with your dog. Follow the correct response with a generous serving of praise. Once you've added the harness to your training, you might want to keep another line attached to the dog's collar so that you can make *gentle* corrections for commands such as "gee" and "haw"—gentle, because you don't want to discourage your dog from moving ahead.

DOCK DIVING

If your dog absolutely adores retrieving and plunging into a pool or pond, this may be the sport for you. It's as exciting to participate in as it is mesmerizing to watch.

To put it in the simplest terms, dock diving involves a dog charging off a dock or pier at speeds of up to 30 miles an hour and heights of up to seven feet above the water . . . and landing in the water with an enormous splash. In competitive dock diving, the goal is achieving the longest leap.

Training her to do all of this is not all that difficult, if you have access to a body of water and a dock or raft. If necessary, introduce her to the water gradually, as described on page 85, and swim together. Then set her up on the dock or raft and use treats or her favorite toy to persuade her to leap into the water. If she's a natural retriever, you'll be able to switch to balls or bumpers in short order, and then you can begin working on the distance of her leaps—a factor that depends, in large part, on the placement of your throws.

Those who go on to enter their dogs in dock-diving competitions say that it combines what they enjoy most. "We like everything about it," says Tom Kallenberger, a former student of mine who participates in competitions, along with his daughter. "Highest on our list is the time we spend training our dogs for the events. But we also enjoy traveling to these events and, once there, spending time with other people who find the sport as much fun as we do."

Tom says that one of the most successful dock divers is a Greyhound-Coonhound cross—not exactly what you would expect. However, retrievers of all kinds are by far the most common breeds at these events.

Tom Kallenberger's dog, Amber, explodes off the pier at a dock-diving event.

To learn more, visit Web sites such as www.dockdogs.com and www.caninewatersports.com. Here, you'll find out everything you want to know about this exciting sport, and have access to state-by-state listings of dock dog clubs—usually a terrific source of training help.

EARTHDOG

If your hyper dog's breed was originally developed to pursue critters in dens or tunnels (known as going to ground), this may be the perfect sport for you. It's open to Dachshunds and any of the smaller terriers—everything from Australians and Bedlingtons to West Highland White Terriers. And it's ideal for any dog who enjoys following quarry, barking, digging, and scratching.

Sound perfect so far? Then check out some earthdog web sites, starting perhaps at www.akc.org or www.terrier.com, for everything from rules and regulations to photos and training tips.

Earthdog training is straightforward, especially with the help of fellow club members. It's mainly a matter of nurturing your dog's natural instinct for detecting and pursuing prey; you'll find lots of friendly and willing help at an earthdog club.

As you both become more proficient, you can enter your dog in tests to earn increasingly difficult earthdog titles.

Terriers are also invited to participate in trailing and locating above-ground quarry. In competition, the dog is judged on her speed and accuracy in a simulated hunting environment. See www.terrier.com for details.

FIELD TRIALS AND HUNTING TESTS

Field trials and hunting tests were developed as ways to demonstrate a sporting dog's innate talent for performing the tasks for which she was bred. Field trials are open to all registered pointers, retrievers, spaniels, Beagles, Basset Hounds, and Dachshunds six months or older. Hunting tests are open to pointers, retrievers, and spaniels.

These trials and tests simulate actual hunting conditions. In field trials, the dogs compete against one another; in hunting tests, they compete against an ideal standard. Levels range from basic to master. For instance, in retriever hunting tests, the basic level covers simple retrieving alone. The master level covers challenging situations, such as multiple birds down, and requires the dog to honor another dog's retrieve—that is, not to retrieve a bird that another dog has been sent to.

A Labrador Retriever delivers the bird to his handler.

The events are tailored to individual breeds. For instance, pointing breeds are run in pairs to demonstrate their ability to find, point, and retrieve game, while spaniels are judged on their ability to hunt, flush, and retrieve birds.

Pat Sullivan is an owner-trainer who got into hunt tests and field trials with Golden Retrievers and now works on these disciplines with Labrador Retrievers. The first time she saw this sport, she realized that although she had good control over her dogs when they were nearby, hunt test and field trial handlers maintain control over dogs who are 200 yards away. She decided to give it a whirl, and before long was hooked.

"I especially enjoy training the dogs, watching them so enthusiastically do the work that they were bred to do," she says. "It takes a lot of time and thought to train an athlete. That's what these dogs are, and it's what I like doing best."

To investigate this sport, you can get in touch with a local gun or hunt club or a breeder, or visit www.akc.org. And if you have a retriever, check out the North American Hunting Retriever Association at www.nahra.org.

FLYBALL

If you value a spirit of cooperation and your hyper dog loves to retrieve and jump hurdles, flyball may be perfect for both of you.

In this sport, teams of four dogs race relay style. Each dog must run down a course studded with hurdles, until she reaches a spring-loaded box. When the dog pounces on a lever on the box, a tennis ball pops out. The dog catches the ball in midair, pivots, and races back over the hurdles again. The next dog is then sent out. The fastest team wins, provided, of course, that all the rules have been followed—including jumping all the hurdles properly and returning with the ball.

This sport was developed in California in the late 1960s and early 1970s, and California remains a flyball hotbed. But, today, the North American Flyball Association lists more than 700 clubs across the United States and Canada. As of this writing, the world record of 15.22 seconds was set in Niagara Falls, Ontario, by a team called Spring Loaded.

To check out everything from rules to eligibility, and to locate a nearby club, visit www.flyball.org.

HERDING

Whether you participate in non-competitive tests or competitive trials, herding events provide a way to measure and enhance a herding dog's instincts, trainability, and utility in the tasks for which she was bred—moving livestock, from sheep, goats, and cattle to ducks and geese.

Performed under the direction of a handler, these events involve a series of increasingly difficult activities and obstacles. Depending on the sponsoring organization, they may be open to any registered Herding-Group breed, as well as to Samoyeds and Rottweilers—or to nonherding and mixed breeds. Titles can be earned, and, in the case of trials, a Herding Championship can be attained by dogs who are able to control even difficult animals in challenging situations.

Your dog must have had previous exposure to working with livestock before entering such events, but you can give her that experience—as well as valuable instruction—by working with herding enthusiasts in your area.

To learn more, do an Internet search for herding lists or groups. Or check out the web site of your breed's parent club or sanctioning bodies such as these:

- American Herding Breed Association, www.ahba-herding.org
- American Kennel Club, www.akc.org
- Australian Shepherd Club of America, www.asca.org
- United States Border Collie Handlers Association, www.usbcha.com

LURE COURSING

Just as scenthounds and sporting breeds are able to demonstrate their talents in field trials, lure coursing gives sighthounds, in particular, the opportunity to show off their ability to catch fleet-footed prey, often over great distances.

This sport allows up to three dogs at a time to chase an artificial lure around a prescribed course over a variety of terrain. Their performance is judged on factors such as speed, enthusiasm, and endurance, as well as the ability to stay close to the lure's "heels." It's a great way to keep a dog mentally and physically fit—and in the process to treat yourself to a most exciting sport.

Lure coursing is open to all the sighthounds, including Afghan Hounds, Basenjis, Borzoi, Greyhounds, Ibizan Hounds, Irish Wolfhounds,

Italian Greyhounds, Pharaoh Hounds, Rhodesian Ridgebacks, Salukis, Scottish Deerhounds, and Whippets. But in addition to "official" events, most clubs host just-for-fun events for many other breeds; herding dogs seem to do especially well, and it seems to be one of the sports that dogs of many different breeds love best.

"It's a thrill for me to watch my dogs excelling at an activity and enjoying it so thoroughly," says Ping Pirrung, an American Sighthound Field Association lure coursing judge who originally got into the sport with Borzoi but currently focuses on Whippets.

Carolyn Mountain, another Whippet owner and ASFA lure coursing judge, agrees wholeheartedly. "My husband and I love to take our dogs lure coursing because it lets them do what they were *bred* to do. And we get to watch them; they are so beautiful and free when they run!"

What sort of canine will excel? "Any dog who has a keenness for the chase that's almost impossible to satisfy," says Carolyn. "This dog will chase anything and everything, from birds to leaves flying around the yard."

Ping suggests that anyone interested in this sport attend an event to watch these athletes at work and to talk to their owners about getting started in the sport. Listings of upcoming events and a downloadable pamphlet on lure coursing are available at www.asfa.org. For information on an upcoming event, click on the host club name and contact information will appear.

Ping Pirrung and her family love to make a weekend of it by taking their Whippets to lure coursing events across the country. This beauty is Wistwind's Wobegone Cavalcade—Cadee to her fans.

The AKC also sanctions lure coursing events. Visit www.akc.org for easy-to-use search tools that will point you to nearby lure-coursing groups.

OBEDIENCE AND RALLY-O

Obedience trials are wonderful demonstrations of control and team-work between owners and dogs of any breed. Curiously, much of the work conflicts with a dog's natural tendencies. For instance, heeling requires her to maintain a very specific position, with nary a reminder or word of praise—and to do so on leash and off, without sniffing the ground, while sitting immediately when her handler halts.

Obedience trials have nevertheless been the most popular per-formance activity for many years. Sadly, these events are currently out of vogue; it takes special bonding, communication, and an extraordi-nary commitment to train a top-performing obedience dog, as well as an amazing level of precision on the part of both handler and dog. Apparently not everyone is up to the task. Which is really a shame, in my opinion. It's an outstanding accomplishment to work through this program to earn a UD, UDX, or OTCh title. In fact, odd as it may seem, perhaps the single most rewarding achievement of my life was earning OTCh titles with my Flat-Coated Retriever, American Staffordshire Terrier, and Japanese Chin—unusual breeds for this sport.

Just for fun, I sent my American Staffordshire Terriers, Oxford (left) and Shaker, over the bar jump in tandem. Jumping is an integral part of advanced obedience.

If you're looking for an organized activity for your hyper dog, I urge you to consider obedience work. Once in competition, your dog will be scored on how she performs a series of exercises. Each time she scores the minimum number of points, she'll be another leg closer to earning an obedience title. What's more, the discipline involved at this level of training can transform virtually any hyper dog into a delightful and totally under-control companion—which will give her a real competitive advantage in learning other sports, such as agility.

Sound a little too formal and labor-intensive for you? Then consider rally-O, a new form of obedience competition that some people find to be more fun, in part because it permits them to give their dogs lots of praise and verbal encouragement. You and your dog work your way along a course from sign to sign; each sign provides specific instructions for maneuvers such as making a simple right turn or doing a 180-degree left pivot, preceded and followed by halts. Between signs, your dog heels at your side.

To learn more, visit www.akc.org and contact a local obedience club.

TERRIER RACES

If you have a terrier who runs as fast as the wind, you might want to look into terrier racing—a sport not unlike horse racing, except for its low entry costs. The dogs chase a lure around a course. There are events for specific breeds, colors, ages, and even sizes, so you can be sure your dog won't be facing dogs with an unfair advantage.

You won't have to worry about your dog's safety in such an event. Every dog wears a muzzle, along with a colored collar for identification during the run for the lure.

Nor will you have to worry about her getting bored. In addition to straight racing on the flat, the dogs race over a series of four steeplechase hurdles placed twenty feet apart.

One of the great advantages of this sport is that you can start training your terrier at home, in your own backyard. For details, including rules, photos, and training tips, visit the Jack Russell Terrier Club of America site at www.terrier.com.

TRACKING, SEARCH AND RESCUE, AND TRAILING

I can't imagine activities with greater potential for helping others than tracking, search and rescue (SAR), and trailing—especially these days. Fortunately, there are many organized events available, and a growing number of clubs and other resources in cities and towns everywhere.

Well-known and well-respected by her fellow trackers, Dorothy Schmidt has been helping dogs and their owners learn to track for more than forty years.

Experts in this field advise knowing what your dog does most effortlessly, and then matching her to the type of training that will take the best advantage of her skills and talents.

For instance, tracking dogs are given a particular article with a human's scent and then are trained to follow that scent while ignoring all others. Or they may be trained to follow a particular footstep or crushed vegetation. Some specialize in urban work; others, in wilderness work.

Scenthounds are obviously a natural choice for this activity. But Dorothy Schmidt is a well-respected Milwaukee-area instructor who has taken another route, helping her Border Collie earn the coveted Champion Tracker (CT) title—the highest in this field. She is currently training a young Border Collie, and can't say enough about this sport.

"I love being outdoors in a field behind a dog who's using his nose to follow a track that's a half hour to five hours old," she says. "To me, it's awesome to watch him work. The dog is in charge and you have to learn to trust him. And once you start tracking, you never look at a field in the same way again."

Any dog can do this work, Dorothy adds. "All dogs have a nose and can smell. All we're doing is teaching them what scent we want them to follow."

There are also a number of search and rescue activities that might be better suited to your hyper dog.

- **Airscenting** is a particularly valuable skill when searchers have no scent article or only a "point last seen" for a missing person.

- A **disaster dog** is trained to find human scent in collapsed buildings and places devastated by natural disasters, such as earthquakes or tornadoes.

- Amazingly, a **water recovery dog** can detect the scent of humans in the water, usually to help narrow dive areas.

And that's just a peek at the possibilities. If you're interested in providing your hyper dog with a worthy way to burn up her energy while enabling you to give something back to the world, this may be a great solution. Look for local trailing, tracking and SAR clubs on the Internet. If you can't find one in your neck of the woods and must start out on your own, read up on the subject, grab some friends, and consider starting a club of your own.

WATER RESCUE TESTS

Imagine a sport that represents a tremendous bonding experience for you and your dog, burns off a ton of her excess energy, and could one day save someone's life. That's precisely what you get when you participate in water rescue dog tests.

Linda Larsen has been involved with Newfoundlands and water rescue dog programs for many years. "The bond created by this activity is wonderful," she says. "It's owner and dog and what you accomplish together as a team. When your dog finishes an exercise, you feel as proud as he or she looks."

The innate talents required are a love of water, retrieving, carrying, and pulling, Linda adds—which explains why she recommends this challenging program for any working dog who enjoys these activities and loves to keep busy.

Although Newfoundlands have traditionally been the breed of choice for water rescue, other breeds can also excel—including Labrador Retrievers and Portuguese Water Dogs. And there are some even more unusual breeds that do very well in this sport.

Barbara Lukacs Grob, a water-rescue dog trainer and the Non-Newfoundland Contact for the Great Lakes Newfoundland Club, says that dogs of any breed, including mixes, can be trained for water work. To prove her point, she notes that the first dog of her own that she trained for this work was an incredible long-coated Chihuahua named Banda of Red Oaks Corner, UDT, WD.

"Banda earned his title pulling the same boat as the Newfies," she reports, "using all the same stewards and equipment except for his 'bumper.' That I hand-sewed to match his size."

The Newfoundland Club of America sponsors an outstanding water-rescue dog testing program—one that's designed not as a competition, but as a training ground to preserve this life-saving capability in the breed. Some regional groups, including the Great Lakes Newfoundland Club, also hold separate tests for any breed, including mixes.

Sam Butler and his Newfoundland, Cassidy, take part in the Great Lakes Water Test in Michigan.

For details, check with your regional Newfoundland Club; contact information can be found at www.newfdogclub.org. For non-Newfie information, get in touch with Barbara Lukacs Grob at Red Oaks Corner, 2508 Meinert Rd., Holton, MI 49425.

Another organization that offers an excellent formal water trial is the Portuguese Water Dog Club of America. You can check out its Water Trial Manual at www.pwdca.org.

WEIGHT PULLING

Weight pulling is a great energy burner that can be done using carts, sleds, or rail carts, depending upon the weather and the available surface. All you need to get started is a great-fitting harness, some weights for conditioning, and a willing dog. Although Huskies, Rottweilers, and Pit Bulls are the most common dogs in these events, breed doesn't matter.

Whether she's pulling a sled or a cart, each dog in a particular weight class pulls the same starting weight, with subsequent pulls being increased in specific increments. A dog who fails to pull a certain weight is done for the event. The one who pulls the most weight wins, and when necessary, speed is the tie-breaker. At a typical event, an individual dog might participate in several contests in a single day.

. . . he lures the dog forward.

Todd Thurber has begun training
Stanley, an American Bulldog, for
weight pulling. After getting
Stanley used to the equipment . . .

Before long, Stanley will be used to dragging around the weights.
Then Todd will teach Stanley to pull a cart.

Those who participate in these competitions say that they're great fun because you meet a lot of interesting people. Your dog burns off a lot of excess energy. And you may even win a prize, such as a 40-pound bag of dog food.

Look for details at www.ukcdogs.com or check with local breeders of the more common weight pulling breeds.

Chapter 9

Extenuating Circumstances

Helping your hyper dog survive life's traumas

··

Over the course of your lives together, you and your hyper dog are bound to encounter potentially upsetting circumstances. But with the right attitude and tools, you'll be able to sail smoothly through just about all of them—*and* transform your dog into a perfect companion in the truest sense of the word.

The right attitude and tools will vary according to the circumstances, of course, and that's what this chapter is about. But there *are* some common denominators to successfully weathering most trials.

- Training: A dog feels more secure when someone else is in charge. Working on obedience training re-establishes you as his authority figure, which will make him more relaxed.

- Exercising: Too often, a dog's exercise routine is the first thing to be set aside in the face of change or crisis. For his sake, do your best to maintain this routine.

- Planning: Whether the subject is moving or traveling, grooming or kenneling, a little planning for the major events in your dog's life can turn potential crises into mere bumps in the road.

- Anticipating trouble: You don't have to worry obsessively, but it doesn't hurt to think about what might go wrong, and plan accordingly. That might mean doing something as simple as bringing along a good supply of water on a summer road trip; it might mean training your dog thoughtfully and thoroughly in preparation for the arrival of a new baby.

Let me give you just one simple example to illustrate how failure to plan and anticipate problems can create difficulties for a hyper dog. Many years ago, when I was just a kid myself, I drove with a relative to pick up her new Brittany pup from a breeder out in the country. It was a glorious Wisconsin summer day, and she had enticed me into the adventure by promising to let me sit in the back seat with the puppy on the return trip. Of course, I eagerly agreed; what more could a kid ask for?

Except that the relative was a chain smoker who preferred to ride with the windows tightly closed, even on such a beautiful day. The sun beating down on the roof of the car was turning the interior into a sauna. And, apparently thinking he was doing us a favor, the breeder had given the pup a good meal before our arrival.

In retrospect, it's no surprise that the puppy spent much of our journey throwing up. Poor planning on the adults' part—as well as my inability to improve the miserable backseat conditions—made the long trip home unnecessarily traumatic for the puppy.

Not to mention me.

ANIMAL COMPANIONS

Sooner or later, most of us at least entertain the notion of bringing in a companion for our hyper dogs. And some of us actually go through with it. It's not a bad idea, in and of itself. Nor is it necessarily a good idea. Its value depends on your unique situation.

Bringing Home Another Dog

Thinking about bringing home another dog? Wonderful! Given a proper introduction and enough supervised time to get used to each other, dogs almost invariably become good friends within a matter of weeks. In fact, you'll want to crate and obedience-train them separately to prevent them from bonding so tightly that they think they have no need of you.

If you have a choice in the matter, experts generally say the safest bet is opposite genders, with both dogs spayed and neutered. But other combinations can work. I've had up to six dogs of both

---

Supervise or Separate

Until you're absolutely sure that your hyper dog and his new canine companion have become fast friends, don't leave them alone together. If you can't be there to supervise them, then make sure they're securely separated.

If you have two dogs, teach them both obedience so that you're able to enforce a command with one dog while you do something with the other. It's a multitasking challenge that's really a lot of fun.

Your command should override any jealousy either dog might feel as you work and play with them separately . . .

. . . but you'll also want to work them together as a team (sometimes called a brace), so that they'll simultaneously obey the same commands.

sexes living together at one time, and have boarded and trained dogs of all sorts over the years.

If you've never introduced two dogs before, you may be amazed at how easy it is. Hyper dogs, in particular, love companionship and will generally welcome another dog—although in his enthusiasm, your hyper hound may overwhelm the less effusive dog. Here are a few suggestions to make the process go as smoothly as possible.

- Once you've brought the new dog home, let her relax and investigate the premises without interference from your hyper dog. Take him out for a good walk and an obedience refresher, and enlist the help of a friend or family member to keep an eye on the new dog while you're occupied. Alternatively, confine your hyper dog in his crate or another room while the new dog explores your home.

- Practice obedience training with your hyper dog in the new dog's presence, using her as a distraction during Sneakaways, downs, stays, comes, and leave-its. This will change his emotional state and establish once again in his mind that it's your house—not his.

- Put your hyper dog in a sit-stay and ignore him while petting, talking to, playing with, and feeding the new dog. Reward him lavishly when he obeys, correct him when he doesn't.

- For their first free-play session together, take them both, on leash, into a medium-size room that's large enough for them to move around freely, but small enough to keep either one from taking off at full speed. Drop their leashes and let them get acquainted.

- Guard against doorway confrontations by closing doors.

- Prevent fights over toys and food by removing anything that makes one of them feel possessive. There are certain items you may never be able to have in your home if you have two dogs—including pigs' ears and rawhide chews. Oh well!

- Expect a certain amount of sniffing, growling, posturing, even biting. As Sue Sternberg explains in her outstanding book, *Successful Dog Adoption*, dogs have their own play styles that can include rough-and-tumble body contact, chasing or being chased, mouth wrestling, and sudden explosions of activity. It's all normal. If your dogs' play styles are incompatible, with one dominating the other, don't give them the opportunity to get too wound up. Neither dog will be psychologically damaged by having the desire for all-out crazy play restrained. And don't worry that you'll have to be forever restrictive; I've found that, over time, dogs tend to adapt their play styles to suit each other.

- If all goes well in your medium-size room, take them outside, still on leash, into a fenced-in area. First practice some obedience. Then, without removing their leashes, set them free to get better acquainted under your watchful eye.

- When your instinct tells you that they're getting along so well that your intervention won't be required, you're probably right; go ahead and remove their leashes.

A pup can make an older dog feel young again. That's what Labrador Retriever Shadow did for my co-author's elderly Basset Hound, Woody, who actually chased his new puppy around between frequent naps.

In the best-case scenario, this entire process—from the time the new dog enters your home until the time both dogs are running around together off leash—could take less than an hour. If you're apprehensive, you may want to take a few days to work through the introductions, continuing with the obedience, supervision, and separation until you feel more confident about how the dogs are reacting to one another.

One other word of warning: As the two dogs bond, they might begin acting like kids, or even worse, teenagers, and fuel each other's desire to make mischief. If you find that they're conspiring to raid the garbage, shred newspapers and magazines, dig up the garden, charge passersby, or embark on any other naughty adventures, check out chapter 10.

Feline Friends

Properly introduced, dogs and cats usually end up being the most devoted of friends. On the other hand, on rare occasions, the combination can be deadly for the cat. So it's not a decision to be made lightly.

Your dog's breed should be a factor in weighing the possibilities. But even if your hyper dog was bred to ferret out small game, the combination may be surprisingly solid. In most cases, you'll simply have to devote some time up front to supervising them both until he's proven his trustworthiness.

When he was young, there wasn't much Shadow enjoyed more than a round or two of Get the Cat. Fortunately, senior Siamese, Sam, shared Shadow's enthusiasm for the game.

A herding breed can be disastrous for felines—or ideal. If the dog is mesmerized by the cat and her movements, he may find it difficult to rein in his herding instinct. That's not necessarily a problem if your cat is confident, bold, and enjoys teasing, playing, and racing around. In fact, such a cat may become his best friend within a few days of their introduction. But a timid cat will be miserable.

My coauthor has found the Oriental breeds, such as Siamese and Burmese, to be particularly well-suited to such cross-species relationships; they're energetic, mischievous, and love to tear around the house with a dog in close pursuit. More docile breeds such as Persians are less enamored of such antics, but that fact may make these cats less interesting to a hyper dog and therefore less likely to be the victims of canine fascination.

The easiest introductions are between puppies and kittens. If they grow up together, they may almost behave like siblings instead of different species. If it's too late for that, try these suggestions.

- Choose a cat who is young enough to be adaptable but old enough to defend herself. Six months is an excellent age. Don't declaw her; instead, either teach her to use a scratching post or get over your need for perfect furniture. Give her a few days to explore her living quarters and get to know the human household members before introducing her to the dog.

- When your new cat is feeling at home, bring her into a room where she'll be able to quickly get out of harm's way if necessary, by racing behind a couch or jumping up on a counter. Then leash your dog and bring him in.

- The cat may well take this opportunity to hide. That's fine. Stay in the room and do some obedience work or tricks. Have a seat and read or watch a little television. Let them get used to being around each other. Stay alert. If the cat decides to dart out of the room, you'll want to be able to short-circuit your dog's pursuit by grabbing or stepping on his leash.

- On the other hand, if she holds her ground, that's great. Let him sniff while you praise the cat soothingly to relax her. Keep him leashed and watch for an opportunity to correct him for overstepping his boundaries or being impolite. Treat the cat like any other distraction; if he's pulling on the leash, do Sneakaways until he's willing to greet her politely.

- You may have to do this twice a day for a week or a month before they're ready to live together peacefully, and it may take many more weeks before they actually become friends. But chances are you'll come home someday to find them cuddled up together, and all your efforts will be worth it.

- In the meantime, until they're at least tolerating each other, use a closed door or baby gate to separate them whenever you're not there to intervene. That way, they'll be able to become accustomed to each other's presence at their own pace.

- Once they're friends, don't stop them from roughhousing with each other. Let them enjoy each other, unless it becomes apparent that one of them isn't enjoying the game.

A New Baby

One of the most traumatic events in the life of a hyper dog is the arrival of a new baby. That's because, inevitably, when the baby arrives, things change for the dog.

Some hyper dogs want nothing more than to be a part of the action by being close to and befriending the mini human being. Some become immediately protective of the infant, making visiting well-wishers at best uncomfortable with their hovering. Some feel neglected and forgotten, often legitimately so as the baby's needs overwhelm the household. And some feel abused, as nervous new parents become increasingly paranoid and snappish every time the dog walks into the room.

Fortunately, there are steps you can take to avoid such situations. Here are some suggestions.

- Plan ahead. My obedience-training school frequently gets calls from expectant couples a few days before their babies are due—couples who seem surprised that their dog didn't somehow outgrow his hyperness over the course of the pregnancy. Late training is better than no training, of course—but it's much better to greet an infant with a hyper dog who is already well under control.

- Take field trips to busy playgrounds to practice your obedience training, and treat the children as distractions to be ignored.

- Get your dog used to your new activities by practicing with a doll—seriously! Have him practice holding the sit-stay while you're diapering, singing to, and feeding the doll, and strapping it into a car seat. Add all the baby accessories you'll soon be toting, from diaper bags to bottles. Teach him to heel alongside you as you push the doll in a stroller. (Your neighbors will think you're crazy, but your dog will display far better manners once you've brought your baby home.)

- Think about buying your baby products well in advance of the happy event. Most of these items have distinctive scents. Open the packages and leave them in the baby's room, allowing your dog to sniff the contents. You can even dab baby powder and oil onto yourself each day. The result? A dog who is desensitized to the smells associated with an infant.

- Designate a comfortable spot to send your dog to when he's in the way. As long as he's not becoming territorial toward your baby, that spot should keep him near you so he will still feel like a valued member of the family. You can set up several such spots in the rooms where you spend the most time—even one in the nursery, if you like.

- Teach him to get off and stay off the furniture.

- Use the Shopping technique to teach him to discriminate between his toys and the baby's things.

- Don't forget how much exercise your dog needs each day. If you run out of time, hire a dog walker or send him to a dog day care facility.

- Look for every possible opportunity to exercise him. Play fetch while you're rocking or feeding the baby, for instance, or grab a few minutes here and there for Play during Training or Rapid-fire Commands.

TODDLERS, CHILDREN, AND TEENS

When a hyper dog meets children, their relationships can be magical—or disastrous. It's largely up to you.

Toddlers

Toddlers can present special problems. On the one hand, they become instantly attractive to a hyper dog because they're constantly dropping food and because they're more or less dog-size. On the other hand, they tend to enjoy pounding on, poking at, and grabbing a dog's hair, ears, and tail—actions that few dogs appreciate. Although many long-suffering individuals tolerate it stoically, not all dogs will. And if they refuse to, your eye-level toddler is in great danger.

Some dogs become inexplicably calm and gentle around little humans. My wild and crazy Rat Terrier, Obey (far left), is instantly transformed into a humble and docile servant in the presence of a young child.

The trick is to desensitize your dog to as many of these things as possible.

- Teach the dog that he doesn't need to pounce on every treat that falls on the floor. How? By practicing the "leave it" command with him as you walk around dropping food.

- Teach him that he doesn't need to be all over someone just because that person is on the floor. Do so by crawling around on the floor yourself, keeping him away using commands such as "wait" or "down," or by using the Magic Marker trick.

- Teach him that sloppy handling is really just petting. Poke and pull at him for a few seconds while you say, "Oh good!" enthusiastically, then follow it up immediately with something he likes to do, such as chasing a ball. Do this often enough, mixing up the pleasurable with actions that could be irritating, and he'll come to see it all as just another way for people to express their love for him.

Children

Children are another story. As soon as they're old enough to understand, teach them to behave in a sensible manner around your hyper dog. Tell them not to hold him against his will, or hug him too hard, or chase him, or run away from him screaming in glee or fear.

Once you have their attention, you can, of course, teach them how to hold the dog properly—as long as you're sure that your instructions and commands will supersede anything that's going on between child and dog. Even then, don't leave your dog unsupervised if any children who aren't yours are around.

As your children get older and you have less time to spend with your dog, take him with you whenever possible—when you're dropping the kids off at school or practice, for example. You could even treat him to some time at a dog park while the kids are busy with their own activities.

Teens

Teenagers present an entirely different challenge—one that I hesitate to bring up, but feel compelled to because it has become alarmingly common. The problem is abuse. Thankfully, instances of deliberately tormenting dogs are not yet epidemic. But boys, especially, may play too rough with a hyper dog who acts as if he can take it. And we are often asked to repair the psychological damage done to dogs who've been tormented in their own yards by kids on the other side of the fence—dogs who, in self-defense, have learned to charge and snarl at passersby in general.

Prevent this problem by refusing to leave your dog outside unsupervised, even if he is fenced in. Be prepared to correct him if he charges and barks, by keeping him on a line that you can jerk or dashing over to spritz Bitter Apple on his lip. And of course, do not tolerate overly rough play on the part of any preteens or teens in your household—or outside of it.

MOVING DAY

There's not much in this life that's more stressful than moving to a new home. That's as true for our dogs as it is for us. And even if *we* manage to remain calm and relaxed throughout the process, our dogs only know that we're tearing down, packing up, and removing the components of their dens. In their minds, this is hardly cause for celebration.

I can't emphasize enough how important it is to:

- Continue exercising and communicating with your hyper dog throughout even the toughest days, via obedience training, games, and tricks.
- Allow him to feel like a part of the process by, for instance, inviting him to sit with you while you pack and taking him along on errands.

If you are too overwhelmed to do these things, please get some help. Hire a dog walker or ask a fellow dog owner to let your dog tag along on their outings.

Once you're in your new home, assume your dog has left all his good habits behind and treat him like he's never had any training at all. That means:

- Whenever possible supervising or umbilical cording him.
- Confining him when you can't pay attention.
- Defining new boundaries for him both inside and outside the house, using the "off" and "wait" commands and the Magic Marker as your primary tools.
- Use the "quiet" command to curtail his barking, so that your new neighbors' first impression of you isn't "the owners of that obnoxious dog who never shuts up."
- Nipping in the bud any astounding new behaviors he has developed, such as jumping on counters or chewing the carpeting (see chapter 10).

Unless you're just moving down the street, you'll want to find a new social network for him as soon as possible, perhaps through a play group, training class, or Yappy Hour.

TRAVELING COMPANION

If you're planning a trip with your dog, you're not alone: An amazing 85 percent of owners report that they travel with their dogs.

To make your experience enjoyable for everyone concerned, you simply need to plan ahead. It starts with packing the right gear—a task that might include the dog's:

- Medications
- Food and treats
- Food and water bowls
- Favorite toys
- Blanket, bed, or collapsible crate
- Brush, comb, and nail clipper
- Leash and collar with identification and rabies tags
- Long line to give him a little more freedom now and then without giving up control
- Bitter Apple to silence any barking
- Health certificates

In addition, pack any specialized equipment you might need—for instance, saddlebags if you plan to do some serious hiking with your hyper dog assuming the role of beast of burden, or collar and leash with reflective lights for walking at night.

Once you've decided what to pack, your mode of transportation is the next issue.

Road Trips

If you're traveling by car, you'll need a canine restraint device such as a harness, carrying bag, or barrier to keep him in the back seat or storage area. This is for his safety and yours. A driver doesn't need the distraction of a hyper dog roaming around the vehicle. In a slam-on-the-brakes event, an unrestrained dog can easily become a projectile capable of hurting himself and his fellow passengers. And in an accident, a loose dog can get out of the car and into traffic—or simply run away.

You may find just the right restraint or barrier at your local pet supply store. Or check out a cutting-edge online store such www.petego.com or a budget-friendly site such as www.petedge.com. If your dog is on the small side, consider a gorgeous pet carrier bag that can be secured with a seat belt in a car (and will transition with ease to the airways)—one with lots of pockets and compartments to hold supplies ranging from brushes to medications. Some even come with wheels so you can pull them like a suitcase—wonderful if you're going to be walking any distance.

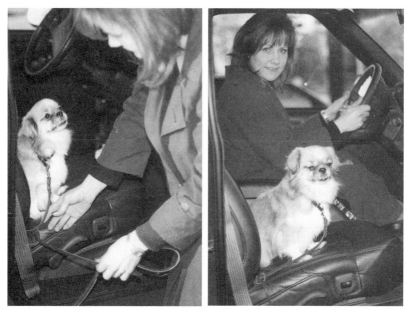

Another option for securing your dog in the car is to tie his leash to the seat belt hardware.

Take some test drives with your dog a week or two before your departure date, using the restraint and gradually building up the distance so that he can get used to the motion gradually. If he gets car sick, ask your vet for advice.

Here are a few suggestions for a peaceful journey once your trip is under way.

- Don't let your dog ride with his head sticking out the window. You don't want him to end up with something embedded in his eye.

- Plan to stop every few hours for a toilet break and a leg stretch.

- Stopping for a meal or some shopping? Park in a shady spot unless it's downright chilly. And if it's at all warm outside, *do not* leave your dog in the car. Even on mild days, it takes just a few minutes for the temperature inside a car to soar to dangerous heights. A cracked window is virtually no help, and a spot that's currently in the shade can become sun-baked in minutes. If you don't want your dog to die of heatstroke, don't *ever* put him at risk.

- Is your dog the sort who barks joyously or menacingly when he's in the car? Simply enforce the "quiet" command, just as you would at home. Even though in the car he is restrained by a device such as a seat belt, barrier, or crate, keep a leash on him specifically for this purpose. If he barks, use the "quiet" command, enforcing it with a leash jerk if necessary. If this doesn't silence him, have someone else drive so you can add a Bitter Apple spritz as a correction until he learns to keep quiet. If your dog causes a ruckus when you exit the car, rush back momentarily to deliver two or three spritzes of Bitter Apple and stay within earshot to repeat if necessary.

- If you'll be looking for places to stay along the way, check out a web site such as www.petswelcome.com or www.BringYourPet.com for dog-friendly hotels, motels, resorts, and campgrounds. More and more places are accepting dogs and cats these days, perhaps a response to competitive pressures or perhaps simply because the demand is growing. That's good news for all of us who would rather stay home than be separated from our dogs.

Flying Dogs

Flying with a hyper dog isn't easy. But then, flying *without* a dog isn't particularly easy these days. Yet every year, thousands of owners venture successfully into the wild blue yonder with their hyper dogs firmly in tow.

If your dog is small enough to fit in a carrier placed under your seat, that's the best route to take. Otherwise he'll have to ride in the cargo hold. The details, and the costs, will vary from airline to airline. Call your airline well in advance of your flight to find out exactly what the alternatives and requirements are. In fact, if your route allows for some flexibility, check with several airlines to find out what their policies are and what kind of accommodations they make for dogs—especially if he'll be forced to ride in the cargo hold.

You'll want to know things like what sort of carrier will be required, what special requirements there are, in terms of everything from health certificates to check-in procedures, and what the airline does to guard against mix-ups and loss. If he'll have to fly as cargo, you'll also want to ask about that environment; confirm that it's lighted and temperature-controlled. Ask what the airline will be willing to do to safeguard his health in the event of unexpected delays.

"What Do You Mean, No Dogs?!?"

It's true that in America, at least, dogs are not welcome in most retail establishments. To which my girlfriend Michelle Naidel says, "So what?"

Michelle has a young Chinese Crested named Milo and an enormously confident attitude. An Olympic-caliber shopper and unabashedly loving dog owner, she takes Milo everywhere—even into the many stores she frequents. She especially likes going to warehouse-size stores like Home Depot or Hancock Fabrics in the winter, because Milo can get lots of exercise shopping at a place like that; as a hairless dog, he doesn't get out much in the cold months.

Michelle and Milo have gone into literally dozens of stores and restaurants together over the years. And yet at only one establishment—a Target—were they ever invited to take their business elsewhere.

Which they promptly did.

Michelle Naidel takes Milo everywhere—even on shopping sprees. Only one store has ever asked them to leave.

Here are some general tips amassed from people who've been there and done that.

- Choose as your travel carrier an ultra-sturdy crate that's big enough to allow your dog to stand up and turn around, and won't open or come apart if it's jostled by turbulence or rough handling.
- Bring the carrier home well ahead of time so you can get him used to spending time in it.
- If possible, book a direct flight so you won't have to add to the stress of changing planes and the potential for mistakes.
- Unless your vet specifically recommends it, don't sedate your dog. It can cause breathing problems when combined with high altitudes.
- My recommendation is to microchip your dog—and, if possible, get his inner thigh tattooed—so you can take his collar off while he's in his carrier. This is controversial, but there are too many things that can go wrong in transit with a collar that's too loose or too snug, and the permanent IDs eliminate the primary need for dressing him in a collar when he's crated.
- Skip the muzzle; if he vomits, he could choke.
- Put huge "LIVE ANIMAL" and "THIS END UP" stickers on his crate.
- Tape a note on the outside of the crate. An airline employee I know recommends saying something like, "Hi! My name is Harold. This is my first flight and I'm friendly but may be a little scared," or whatever is appropriate for your dog. Include any special care requirements, as well as origin and destination. Apparently, such notes are almost always read.
- If he's traveling in the cargo hold, watch to make sure he's been loaded onto the plane. If you have to change planes and you can't actually see the transfer process, ask a flight attendant for confirmation that he has been moved to your flight.
- Even during more moderate weather, if you run into unexpected delays at the gate or on the runway, ask the flight attendant to get the temperature in the cargo area checked, and to have your dog taken out if that temperature is approaching dangerous levels.

To Board or Not to Board?

Many people believe that a hyper dog is better off staying at home when they're away, with a pet sitter stopping in a couple of times a day or, even better, staying at their home for the duration. Sounds like the most comfortable solution, doesn't it? But in reality, it can be a lonely one for your dog.

The hubbub of a kennel may be a far better fit for a hyper dog because of the mental stimulation it offers. Just make sure you choose the right facility, one with a well-thought-out and generous schedule of exercise and interaction. You may be surprised to find that your dog enjoys his time as a boarder so thoroughly that he bounds happily in the door on subsequent visits.

Boarding at a good kennel means your dog will be handled by dog experts who understand canine health, can accommodate special medical needs, and know how to spot and treat impending problems before they have a chance to become serious. They wear "trouble detectors" at all times, especially when walking their clients; they remain aware of their surroundings and always exercise the appropriate amount of caution. And they may even reinforce your training efforts.

In short, it's highly unusual for an owner to return to disaster if the dog has been boarded in a top-quality kennel. It is not so unusual for the owner who leaves his pet at home.

Boarding at a kennel can give a hyper dog the mental and physical stimulation he craves, and may therefore be preferable to leaving him at home with a dog sitter.

That's not to say you should board your hyper dog if you have an excellent alternative. Given enough time and attention from a sitter with dog-handling experience, most dogs *would* prefer to stay home, and some amateur sitters are better dog handlers than the average owner.

Choosing the Right Professionals

Unless you've heard glowing reports from a fellow dog owner about a particular kennel, you'll have to do some homework.

- Ask everyone you know, including your vet and the clinic staff, for recommendations.
- Narrow the field down to a few choices and check them out in person. Ask for a tour of the facilities and make notes about cleanliness, exercise facilities, feeding and exercise schedules, willingness to accommodate special needs, the policy on handling emergencies, and the overall attitude and knowledge of the staff.
- Ask what is done to protect your dog from contagious diseases. For instance, does the kennel require vaccinations against kennel cough? If so, great!
- Ask for references, and check them.
- Finally, call the Better Business Bureau to check out your top choices. Ask if there are any pending or previous complaints or disputes that might affect your decision.

You'll want to take similar care in interviewing and hiring in-home pet sitters. Find out what sort of experience they have, with what breeds of dogs. Take note of how they interact with your pet and how knowledgeable they seem to be about canine care. Find out how willing they are to accommodate your preferred schedule for feeding and toileting. Ask how much time they would spend in your home during each visit, playing with and loving your dog. And ask them what they'll do in the event of an emergency.

So far so good? Then ask for and follow up on their references.

If you take these steps, you'll be able to relax in the knowledge that you're doing the best you can for your dog. I always feel most secure leaving my dogs in the hands of people who know what they're doing, and are willing to do what they know is right rather than just what I tell them to do. I also appreciate handlers who won't ever be too permissive or oblivious to the very real dangers that can arise in caring for a dog.

In Case of Emergency . . .

Chances are there won't be any major problems. But it's important to know what your hyper dog's caregivers will do if something disastrous happens. Will they be willing to take your dog to a vet—ideally, your vet—in the event of an emergency? If so, will they get in touch with you and keep you posted? Will they cover any bills until you get back, or will you need to leave your credit card information and spending limits on file with their vet of choice?

GOOD GROOMING

If bathing and clipping strike horror into your hyper dog, take heart: Any dog can learn to cooperate with and even love being groomed.

The first thing to do is to get your dog used to the touching and restraint associated with grooming. He has to at least tolerate, and perhaps even welcome, your handling of his head, feet, legs, and tail.

Put him on a table or in a sit-stay or down-stay on the floor—or use the Dead Dog trick. Then, holding his collar so you're ready to jerk it if necessary to settle him down, examine him from head to toe. Look in his eyes, ears, and mouth. Examine his feet, feeling the toes, pads, and nails. Run your hands along his legs, belly, and tail. Once he can stay calmly during all that touching—after one session or a dozen, depending on the dog—he should allow you to hold any part of his body without pulling away.

Ideally, you should start practicing this type of touching when he's very young. Otherwise, you may find yourself having to wrestle him to the floor every time you want to trim his nails—which means that it's always a traumatic experience for both of you.

Spend some time desensitizing your hyper dog to head-to-toe handling, and he'll be a favorite at the groomer's place as well as the vet's office.

Next, teach him to stand obediently on a table or platform and secure him with a professional groomer's noose or collar-and-leash combo so that he can begin getting used to being tethered by an invisible overhead handler. Praise him soothingly if he stands patiently for you.

When he is tolerating these conditions well, give him a good brushing, focusing at first on the areas that seem to give him the most pleasure. If he has long hair, make sure you brush the coat all the way down to the skin. A slicker brush—one with fine pins bent at a 45-degree angle—is a great tool for this. Make sure to remove debris and mats from the head, muzzle, and underbody.

Next, desensitize him to the noise and air of blow drying by introducing a hair dryer to the situation. Don't point the dryer at him until he's become oblivious to the noise it makes. Even then, begin with a low setting. If he'll need clipping, use the dryer to simulate the noise and vibration of a clipper.

Finally, get him used to having his nails clipped or ground—something you'll probably need to do routinely, at least every couple of weeks. If you've never clipped a dog's nails, ask your vet to show you how, or consult a grooming

Although it's nice to have a professional grooming table, complete with grooming arm . . .

. . . you don't need a fancy setup—just a collar, a leash, and a hook or a pipe to tie it to, decent lighting, and a platform such as the top of a freezer, washer, or dryer. These simple tools will help your dog cooperate and will facilitate thorough grooming.

book or the Internet. One of the best articles I've seen about this is at www.vetmed.wsu.edu/clientED/dog_nails.asp.

Once he's handling all of these steps stoically, he'll be ready for some serious grooming. Many owners take their dogs to professionals. If you don't want to spend the money, and enjoy the bonding that's a fringe benefit of grooming, go ahead and do it yourself. Here's an overview of how to make it a decent experience for everyone concerned.

Baths Without the Splish-Splash

The first step is that dreaded doggie bath. It's true that some hyper dogs are terrified of being bathed. But most tolerate it just fine, and some really enjoy it.

Here's what you'll need.

- Shampoo, ideally purchased from a pet-supply store or pet catalog, since some of the grocery store brands cause severe dandruff on certain dogs
- Cream rinse if your dog has long hair
- A hose and sprayer that will fit securely on the faucet you'll be using
- Lots of towels
- The dog's collar and leash

If you need to buy any of these things, check out some good, economical sources such as www.petedge.com and www.leather brothers.com.

If you have access to a stationary tub (the sort of utilitarian raised tub that's often found in basements), I strongly recommend that you use it rather than a bathtub. The lighting will be better, the elevation will be easier on your back, and you'll be able to tie the leash to a nearby pipe. Best of all, you'll be able to attach the sprayer hose securely to the faucet with a standard hose fitting, so it won't go flying off in the middle of that all-important rinse.

An excellent alternative, becoming more widely available with every passing year, is a self-serve dog wash. The equipment, towels, and mess stay where they belong, permanently out of your home.

Lift or help your dog into the tub and tie his leash to something solid nearby, such as a pipe. Don't leave any slack in the leash; once he figures out that there's nowhere to go, he will settle down for the duration. Keeping the water pressure quite low and the sprayer head close to his body, get him wet.

To wash the head, muzzle, and ears, reduce the water pressure, keep the nozzle against the dog's skin and be ultraconservative with your application of shampoo. If the dog's head isn't stinky or dirty, skip it and wash him from the neck back. Lather up every inch of his body to the top of his neck. Finally, rinse rinse rinse; professional groomers say to rinse until you're sure your dog is squeaky clean, and then rinse him again.

It can be tough to bathe a dog thoroughly in a sink, but it will do in a pinch if your dog is very small.

The Finishing Touches

Use your hands to gently squeeze out the excess water. Then wrap him in towels and rub him down to dry him off.

Then it's back to work. Position him on your grooming table or platform, using the noose or collar-and-leash combo to keep him still, and follow the steps appropriate to his breed or coat type to blow dry, brush, clean his ears, and possibly trim his coat.

You'll find a number of good books on breed-specific or general grooming at your local bookstore. If your hyper dog is a mixed breed, he'll probably look his handsome best if you follow the recommendations for the breed he most closely resembles.

AT THE VET'S OFFICE

For many hyper dogs and their owners, a trip to the veterinarian is a traumatic experience. But it doesn't have to be. Basic obedience training

Going to the vet's office? The time to start putting your hyper dog's obedience skills to work is before you even open the clinic door.

The waiting room scale is an excellent place to showcase your dog's obedience skills.

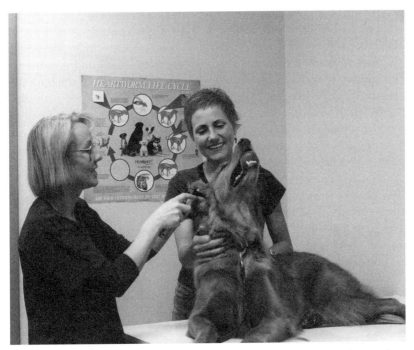

Veterinarians really appreciate a dog who remains relaxed and compliant throughout the exam.

can transform these visits into tolerable and even pleasant experiences—especially since vets and technicians tend to lavish attention and praise on well-behaved dogs.

These visits also present you with a great opportunity to practice obedience in the presence of often formidable distractions, including the ruckus created by untrained dogs.

RE-HOMING YOUR DOG

Okay, this is a horrid subject. Unfortunately, it sometimes becomes necessary, for whatever reason—a change of landlord, a cross-country move, illness, a change in one's economic fortunes—the folks at animal shelters around the world have heard it all.

The common denominator is how heartbreaking it is to hand one's beloved dog over to others—especially when he's a hyper dog with personality-plus, and especially when you don't know what his fate will be. But if you have to do it, you have to do it.

Fortunately, there are some things you can do to help ensure he has a happy future with someone else. First and foremost is training. A polite and responsive dog will be miles ahead of his competition when it comes to landing desirable new owners. Second is good grooming. Few people want to adopt a project. Get him looking and smelling his beautiful best before you do anything.

Next, decide on your course of action.

For instance, you can post ads in the local newspaper or on Internet sites whose purpose is to bring pets together with prospective owners. You can put up signs at work, local supermarkets, pet stores, vet clinics, dog-training studios, and animal shelters. And if he's a purebred, you can list him with his breed's rescue group or a purebred dog-rescue group, or enlist the help of his breeder.

Even if your dog is a mutt, you can point out that he's a well-trained and mature mutt, writing up a heart-warming description of his personality and the breed he most resembles. You can tell everyone you know about this great dog you're forced to give up—including your vet, who may know of a great owner who recently lost a beloved dog and might be ready to welcome a well-trained new canine into his or her life.

Through these efforts, you may soon be interviewing prospective owners. Do not hesitate to (politely) grill them. Check out the applications used by your local animal shelter and follow their pattern. Or simply use common sense. Be sure to ask:

- About family members and whether everyone wants him
- If they rent, and if so, if they're allowed to have a dog; call to confirm
- About their previous dog experience
- What vet they use, and call that vet, if possible, to find out if he or she would recommend these people as good owners
- How they feel about crating and obedience training

Bend over backward to find the best possible home for your dog, and you'll never have to beat yourself up for giving him up. You'll be giving him a second chance at living the life of Reilly. And in his own way, he'll be forever grateful to you if you succeed.

Chapter 10

Hyper Troubleshooting

```
Solutions  central
```
....

I f you need a quick fix for a particular hyper dog problem, you've come to the right place. This chapter includes in-a-nutshell solutions to some of the most common, and often the most intractable, problems a hyper dog can raise.

But before you look for solutions to the particular problems you're facing, take a moment to reflect on three guidelines that are of critical importance to raising a hyper dog.

GUIDELINE 1: DON'T DESPAIR

No matter how out of control your hyper dog may seem, rest assured that the situation is *not* hopeless. Remember that every day is a new learning experience for her. If she was able to pick up some obnoxious new behavior, she is still capable of learning; all you have to do is teach her to leave that particular behavior behind and replace it with something that is acceptable.

That might mean backing up a step or two to be more strict with her until the problem is resolved—for example, by increasing the amount of time she spends confined to prevent her from pursuing some particularly destructive or dangerous habit.

Or it might mean adapting your routines or environment to nip a benign behavior in the bud. Whether the solution to your particular problems falls into either of these extremes or somewhere in between, stay the course. The suggestions in this chapter will help you do just that.

A Taste for Tissues

Some years ago, my very-well-trained, polite, 8-year-old Whippet, Orbit, stayed with my mother for a few weeks while I was on the road giving seminars. All was well when Orbit and I returned home to our condo, happy to be together once again—until I started noticing tissues on the floor every time I turned around. I was perplexed: This was definitely not like my Orbit.

Except, as it turned out, it *was*. She'd picked up the habit of raiding wastebaskets at my mother's home. Not that there was anything especially exciting in them, but it was a new environment for her and she didn't know she was supposed to stay out of the garbage there, too. So in a matter of weeks, she'd developed a taste for tissues and a brand new habit.

I could have trained her to drop this habit by setting her up and correcting her. But because it was a relatively benign behavior and because it was easy enough to stop it by putting my wastebaskets behind closed cabinet doors, that's what I decided to do. Set-ups and stakeouts can take a lot of time, and in this case it was easier to change the environment than to change Orbit.

GUIDELINE 2: BE DILIGENT

Don't make the mistake of thinking that one class will be enough to transform a wild thing into a perfectly trained dog. And don't think that a quick refresher will be enough to remind a rebellious backslider of her manners. In both cases, it's likely that you'll have to invest some time and effort to achieve the desired results.

Say, for instance, that your hyper dog is close to being perfectly housebroken. But every once in a while she leaves another surprise for you in the corner of the living room (usually, within 24 hours of your thinking, "Finally, I have a housebroken dog!" and often five minutes after company has arrived).

When this happens, it's time to face the fact that your hyper dog is not really housebroken at all—and to relaunch the process of combining crating, supervision, chant, and praise prescribed under Housebreaking Issues below, even if it's your second or third attempt.

GUIDELINE 3: TRUST YOUR INSTINCTS

Whether you're starting from scratch or are in repair mode, at some point you'll have to determine when the problem in question has been solved.

Trust your instincts. You'll know in your gut when it's safe to resume life as you once knew it—or when it's time to accept any compromises you've made as permanent accommodations to eliminate the possibility of hyper-misbehavior.

PROBLEMS AND SOLUTIONS, FROM A TO Z

Nearly 3,000 years ago, King Solomon observed that there's nothing new under the sun. That's certainly true of hyper dogs, at least in my experience. The details may change, but the problems their owners bring to my dog-training school can generally be traced to a handful of common misbehaviors.

Fortunately, even those that seem the most intractable can be eliminated or managed fairly quickly by combining the right troubleshooting techniques with some time and effort. This section will provide you with the most important of these techniques; add the necessary time and effort, and you should begin seeing progress in short order.

But if your goal is one-command control over a truly outstanding canine companion, don't stop here. Your hyper dog will need the discipline and bonding that result only from the obedience training and focused exercise described in the preceding chapters.

Regain Control with Rapid-fire Commands

Next to the Sneakaway, perhaps the most valuable tool for re-establishing authority over an out-of-control hyper dog is Rapid-fire Commands.

With your dog leashed, launch into a series of random commands and tricks, delivered almost as quickly as she can comply. Use sit, down, stay, come, heel, sit up, and whatever else you have in your arsenal at the moment, mixing them up and repeating as much as necessary to get her attention focused exclusively on you.

It's critical that you instill a sense of great urgency in this exercise. Insist that your dog respond instantly to each command; enforce it rather than waiting patiently for her to comply. Command her full attention by praising her and immediately launching into the next command.

When you're sure you have her full attention, praise her, give her a chin-touch okay and do something else—return to your guests or chores or play a game of ball with her. In the unlikely event that she decides to return to the behavior that made the Rapid-fire Commands necessary, repeat the exercise.

Aggression

Some dogs seem to be prone to aggressive behavior toward other animals, while others are prone to aggression toward people. If your dog has either of these problems, you're going to have to address it.

You should be 90 percent of the way there if you commit yourself to thorough obedience training, especially around distractions. Once you've achieved one-command control over your dog, your authority will supersede any action she's thinking about taking—even aggressive action.

If yours is one of the rare dogs whose aggression is not mitigated by solid basic training, no book in the world is going to help you deal with this problem. You will need to get professional help from a dog trainer with a proven record of success in dealing with the type of aggression your dog is exhibiting.

Barking and Baying

Hyper dogs are especially prone to expressing themselves orally—and left unchecked, it's practically guaranteed to drive you (and perhaps your neighbors) up the wall.

The solution is the "quiet" command. Teach it early and enforce it relentlessly, and you shouldn't have a problem with inappropriate noise-making.

If this technique doesn't do the trick, you may have to become a little more hands-on. Give her one sharp jerk or a series of light jerks on the collar as you simultaneously close your other hand around her muzzle. Then as she quiets down, lighten your grip on both collar and muzzle while keeping your hands in place; you'll most likely have to reissue the correction. She may struggle, but don't give in. And don't say "quiet" again. In this, as in everything else related to dog training, your goal is one-command control.

When she is silent, praise her and release her muzzle. You may need to repeat this several times before she acknowledges defeat by staying quiet.

Begging

At first, it may seem kind of cute when your hyper dog sits by your side during meals, gazing up at your with her big, sad, hungry eyes. You might even be tempted to reward her for being so adorable by giving her a little something straight from your plate.

Stop! Don't even think about it!

In the first place, most people feel pretty uncomfortable eating with a dog staring up at them. So unless you plan to banish dinner guests permanently from your home, you'll want to nip this behavior in the bud.

Second, if you don't head off this kind of begging—worse, if you actually encourage it—those pitiful stares can quickly escalate into more vocal and aggressive begging.

The easiest solution is to keep your hyper dog from getting started with this bad habit in the first place—or to correct it if it's already a problem. Resolve never ever to feed her people food. If you simply cannot resist, wait until your meal is over and then give her a tiny taste in her own bowl. Stop any barking, whining, or jumping up with the suggestions in this chapter. And if the sitting and staring bothers you, send the dog away from the table, perhaps to her bed or crate, or use the Magic Marker trick.

An important corollary: If you're sitting at your dinner table, don't invite your dog to jump up in your lap—not even if you've finished your meal. And don't let your guests do so, either. Canine cuddling should take place away from the table!

Biting, Nipping, Mouthing

If your hyper dog begins using her mouth for anything other than eating, drinking, and making an occasional comment or two, you'll want to stop this behavior. Biting, nipping, and mouthing are never acceptable.

Begin by checking on how others in your household are interacting with her. Does anyone play roughly with her, growling, shoving, grabbing her fur, or tugging teasingly on her tail? If so, that may be the problem. It's wonderful to play with your dog, but do so by acting and talking silly, dancing around, tossing toys, and giving her playful little pushes at most. Eliminating any more aggressive play with humans may solve the problem instantly. If that's not the problem, keep your dog leashed even in the house and be ready to substitute basic obedience commands when she begins biting, nipping, or mouthing you. When she's following your commands, you can release her and give her an acceptable toy or nylon bone to satisfy her oral cravings.

Chasing, Stalking, Predatory Behavior

Some dogs are born to pursue other creatures—terriers, herding dogs, and hounds, for instance, were bred for such tasks, and without training can be counted on to take off instinctively after anything that moves.

Freedom Is Habit-Forming

Even seemingly well-trained dogs have been known to back-slide when powerful temptations arise, as my trainer friend Donna Koehn can testify.

Donna has three Australian Shepherds—an under-2 male named Levi and 1- and 5-year-old females. Although they were never unsupervised outdoors, she frequently took them outside her country home unleashed.

And then one day, with only Donna's daughter, Jessie, keeping an eye on them, Levi decided it would be fun to chase the deer that had wandered into his field of vision. He took off, the female Aussies in pursuit.

Jessie followed in her car and eventually found Levi standing on the bank of a nearby highway, his pads raw and bleeding. She found one of the females a ways down the road, where several drivers had pulled over to try to coax her into the safety of their vehicles. And she found the third dog waiting for them at home.

A couple of days later, despite his tender, bandaged paws, Levi and the girls shocked Donna by taking off once again, this time when they were under Donna's supervision.

She was able to gruffly call them back again, but she didn't need any more convincing that they were not as well-trained as she thought; she grabbed her training equipment and worked on remedial boundary skills for many weeks before allowing them off-leash freedom again. (For information on boundary training, see the *Amiable Basic Handbook* and *Amiable Basic* DVD, both available from the online store at www.dogclass.com.)

Levi's story is a good demonstration of how easily the seed of rebellion can be planted in a dog who hasn't been thoroughly tested against extreme temptations—and how quickly such disobedience can become a habit, regardless of a dog's training history.

Some dogs, though, have been programmed to chase by their owners. "Where's the squirrel?" such people will ask repeatedly in an excited whisper, thinking that it's a riot to watch Spot chasing a "tree rat" up into the old oak.

But it's not a riot, and in fact, it's not a good idea at all. I've seen this sort of encouragement backfire when hyper dogs who've been encouraged to chase or stalk end up throwing themselves through a screen or windowpane in pursuit of a humble chipmunk.

Whatever you do, don't charge your dog's batteries. And if she begins chasing, stalking, or exhibiting predatory behavior on her own, nip it in the bud with a whole-hearted campaign of Sneakaways to build her self-control.

In the meantime, if you find yourself outside with her off-leash and see her tensing in that "I've seen something and I'm about to launch myself after it" pose, don't wait: Get her attention with a sharp "hey!" or "ach ach," exclaim "good!" when she acknowledges you, and run like the wind away from her—seriously, just as fast as your legs will carry you. If possible, disappear around a corner. If all is right with the world, she will follow you in hot pursuit, forgetting entirely the prey that moments earlier meant the world to her.

Keep in mind that this is an emergency measure only—not a substitute for keeping her leashed until you have total control over her off leash.

Chewing

Almost anyone who has ever had a puppy has lost some favorite items to chewing. And puppies are not the only culprits.

Fortunately, what seems like an intractable habit is not really all that hard to break. A combination of basic training, supervision, and confinement will go a long way toward solving the problem. Providing appropriate toys will help, as will using the Shopping technique to teach her to discriminate between her things and yours.

Make a commitment to keeping her favorite contraband well out of reach. And, as the finishing touch, keep your Bitter Apple spray handy so that if you catch her in the act, you can respond swiftly with a jerk of the collar and a spritz on the lipline.

Digging and Scratching

Digging is not only a lot of fun for some dogs, it can also be a survival mechanism. They do it to make a cool or warm place to lie down, to create a nest, or to investigate interesting smells in the soil.

That's why this is one of the few problems that cannot be solved strictly by thorough basic training; the best you can hope for on that score is that the training will relieve the boredom that can sometimes exacerbate this behavior.

If your hyper dog's a digger, do your best to prevent this behavior. When you can't supervise her, leave her on an undiggable surface—a concrete run or patio, for example. Be sure to make it comfortable, providing fresh water and shelter from heat, cold, wind, and rain. In the meantime, give her plenty of exercise so that she doesn't turn to digging to burn off excess energy.

Correcting this behavior requires extreme vigilance. You have to catch her the moment she starts digging, and then startle her without saying a word.

You can do so by tossing a shaker can at her (a soda can containing eight pennies, taped closed if it makes you feel more secure, although the coins probably won't fall out on their own). If you live in a two-story house, toss it from a second-story window for maximum effectiveness. Alternatively, make a *loud* noise. A boat horn is an inexpensive and effective tool, but out of respect for your neighbors, use it only if you're in a rural area.

The Canine Gardener

If you're a gardener with a young or new hyper dog, beware: Chances are she's going to observe you digging in your flower beds and follow suit the moment your back is turned—wrapping up each extraction by gobbling down as much of the plant as possible before you discover your loss.

That's how my coauthor's Labrador Retriever, Shadow, spent much of the first couple of summers of his life. He was partial to plants she'd just patted firmly into place—and especially fond of taking off with the rarer (and therefore more expensive)

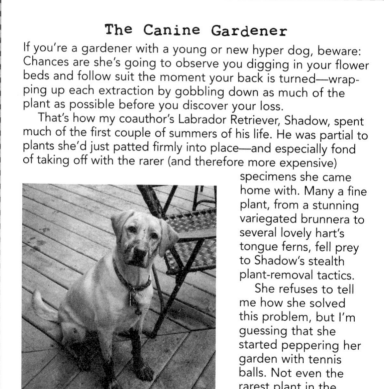

specimens she came home with. Many a fine plant, from a stunning variegated brunnera to several lovely hart's tongue ferns, fell prey to Shadow's stealth plant-removal tactics.

She refuses to tell me how she solved this problem, but I'm guessing that she started peppering her garden with tennis balls. Not even the rarest plant in the world can capture the attention of this particular Lab if there's a tennis ball anywhere in the vicinity.

Until he discovered the joys of tennis balls, my coauthor's Lab, Shadow, loved to help out in the garden.

Alternatively, attach a light line before setting her free and give it a silent jerk if she starts to dig. If she's tied out, attach a second line that's long enough for you to hold and jerk if she starts digging.

Don't give up. While it's a tough behavior to stop permanently, and relapses may well occur, some persistent people ultimately have success with these techniques.

You can take a similar approach to scratching at the door—fortunately, a much easier problem to solve. Again, the key is to catch her in the act and startle her.

If she scratches to get to you when you're on opposite sides of the door, you can set her up by leashing her and standing on the other side of the door, leaving it open just enough so that the leash can slide but not so much that she can put her nose into the opening. Then, when she starts scratching, jerk the leash. And again, if you live in a two-story house, you have another good option if she's outside scratching to get in: Dash upstairs with a shaker can and toss it out the window at her.

If she scratches when you're both inside or both outside, leave her leashed and use a jerk to startle her, or toss a shaker can at her.

Eating Inedibles

Left to their own devices, dogs will eat all kinds of disgusting things, from dead rodents to feces. If your dog will be outside unsupervised, you can bet that someday she's going to come inside and upchuck something revolting, probably on your best carpet.

It's obviously best to prevent these occurrences. Begin by policing her area frequently and removing anything you don't want her to grab. Even then, you may need to take some extra steps—for instance, putting her on a light line when she's headed outside, so that if she picks up anything she shouldn't, you can use the "drop it" command or quickly walk down the line to give her a spritz of Bitter Apple.

Excitability

Once she's excited, even a well-trained hyper dog can be pretty difficult to control. Fortunately, there's a relatively easy fix called Play during Training—a way to develop an emotional on-off switch in your dog, so she can go from all-out play to all-out obedience almost instantly.

To get started, leash her and do everything possible to get her delirious with excitement. Use toys, dancing around, and intense praise, encouraging her to join you in your escapades.

Catch Me If You Can

Have you ever found yourself trying to catch a hyper dog who keeps dancing just out of your reach? It doesn't matter how the situation arose, whether you let her off leash or someone allowed her to escape through an open door. Her refusal to let you catch her can be very frustrating.

The most important thing to remember in this situation is not to get grabby. If you reach for her, she'll just dance away again, thinking you've got a fine game going here.

Instead, try making a sharp sound such as "hey!" or "ach ach" to get her full attention on you and away from her rebellion, even for a split second. Then call "come" and run away from her as fast as you can.

If she doesn't respond, there's not much you can do about it. But she probably will come. In that case, stop suddenly to face her, kneel, and praise her enthusiastically as she gallops toward you. Keep your hands close to your body and squat down, telling her how very smart and good she is. Don't lift a hand until she gets very close to you; then scratch her ear or throat, praise her some more, and finally take her collar in hand.

The immediate problem solved, you'll want to get to work on that all-important "come" command just as soon as possible.

As soon as she's pretty much out of control, stop playing and put her into a sit-stay. Praise her profusely for obeying, even if you have to give her some guidance. Then move around and start tossing distractions such as toys and food, using a fast, sure correction whenever necessary. After a minute or two, return to her, praise her, release her with a chin-touch okay, and play with her again.

Next, heel her around and over the food and toys you just tossed around, and then stop and enforce the automatic sit. Distract her by kicking one of the toys away. Then release her with a "chin-touch okay" and let her go. Then take it away from her and start a rousing game of keep-away. Toss in a command now and then before returning to play.

She'll soon realize that the faster she obeys your commands, the sooner she'll get to play again; in other words, playing becomes a reward for obedience. And best of all, she'll develop that on-off switch that enables an out-of-control dog to transform herself instantly into the epitome of the well-trained canine.

Housetraining Issues

Most dogs won't be rock-solid housetrained until they're at least 7 months old. And for some breeds, that happy day may be delayed until they're almost a year. Whatever her age, until that day arrives, treat your hyper dog as if she's not housetrained at all. That means:

- When you're able to, keep a constant eye on her or umbilical cord her.
- Crate her when you're unable to supervise her.
- Take her outside immediately before and after crating, as well as after meals at the intervals she seems programmed for. Select a designated toileting area so she always knows what's expected of her when you take her there.
- Once outside, launch into a stimulating chant, such as "potty hurry up" or "sis boom bah," the moment she starts to relieve herself. Then praise her when she's finished.
- To help her gain control over her bowels and bladder, feed her a measured amount of dog food on a regular schedule and consider limiting her access to water to specific times that will fit in with scheduled play and potty outings. But consult your veterinarian to confirm that this plan is consistent with his or her recommendations.
- When she's uncrated and roaming free in your home, keep a leash and collar on her and watch her constantly. The moment she starts sniffing around or squatting, snap the leash to distract her and rush her out to the designated toileting area.

What this does *not* mean—ever—is punishing her after the fact in any way. That can be both counterproductive and cruel.

While you're working toward getting your hyper dog thoroughly housetrained, take a few moments to reflect on the housetraining myths that have set so many dog owners up for failure over the years.

- "A well-trained dog will let you know when she needs to go potty." Not true. She may let you know when she wants to go outside, but that may or may not be because she needs to eliminate. And if you let her out every time she sounds the alarm, you become her automatic doorman and she never develops the ability to hold it. Instead of teaching your hyper dog to alert you, use supervision and a carefully planned schedule of "potty outside" breaks to teach her self-control and extend her capacity to hold it.

- "Leave her out long enough and she won't go inside." This isn't necessarily true, either. You'll just be giving her more time to sniff around, watch the birdfeeder, chase a few squirrels, and bark at the neighbors.

- "She just piddled. She's good to come in." Not necessarily. Some hyper dogs—especially puppies and older dogs—need to urinate or defecate more than once during a single outing. Go ahead and bring her in, but unless she's rock solid, don't leave her unsupervised until you're 100 percent sure of her.

There are several special housetraining issues you should be aware of. The first is the possibility that a hyper dog's housetraining problem is actually a medical issue. Medications can alter a dog's capacity or elimination habits, for instance. And dogs can develop bladder and kidney infections fairly easily, so if you're stuck, check with your vet. The cure is usually simple, inexpensive, and amazingly effective.

The second issue is marking by male dogs. An effective way to stop this behavior is to set your dog up: Rub a towel on another dog and drape it over a chair or sofa. Then put your dog on a light line and spy on him as he wanders into the room. Once he sniffs the towel, he'll want to mark the territory as his own. Snap the line before he lifts his leg.

Submissive urination is a third issue. It's a problem with many puppies and some breeds that are prone to uncontrollably leaking urine when they're feeling especially emotional—for instance, when a visitor arrives. This problem can't be eliminated, but you can minimize it by getting the dog to focus on your commands, rather than on her emotions, in situations where she would ordinarily leak. It's also important to avoid eye contact, touching, and talking to her when she's in an emotional state, and to keep your entrances, and your guests, as calm and emotionless as possible.

Howling

See Barking and Baying.

Jumping Up

Does your dog greet visitors by jumping on them? Does she leap up on your furniture against your wishes, or spend a lot of time and energy trying to get at whatever might be on your kitchen counters?

Jumping up is a bad habit you can stop in fairly short order with the "off" command. And in the case of jumping up on guests, consider adding the Magic Marker trick to your repertoire, or for a small dog, platform training; they have the added advantage of impressing visitors!

Pacing

Pacing is normally a nervous habit that indicates your dog is feeling uneasy. Often, it's the result of insufficient exercise—an issue that's ordinarily easy to resolve, even if that means hiring someone to walk her. It could be boredom, which might be alleviated with a new chew toy or periodic bursts of Play during Training. Or it might be that she doesn't have a comfortable place to sleep and still be near you; that, too, is easy to rectify.

Be aware, however, that sudden-onset pacing could be an indication that the dog is in pain, so it's a good idea to check with your vet.

Phobias

If you're the owner of a hyper dog who's terrified of noises such as sirens or fireworks. . . who flips out at the very thought of entering an elevator or climbing an open-backed stairway. . . who sees monsters in every manhole, grate, dumpster, or wheelchair she encounters. . . you probably feel as if you have quite a problem on your hands—especially if you live in the city, where your dog should be basking in the abundant mental and social stimulation of urban life instead of being consumed with fear.

Fortunately, giving her the courage she needs to face such traumas is usually easier than you might think. Here's the scoop.

First, show her how calm, relaxed, and unemotional you are in the face of this incredible danger. Second, use basic obedience commands to get her to focus on you instead of her fear. And third, distract her with treats and happy talk.

Start by setting your dog up to face the object of her fear. If the threat is something that you can't really re-create—for instance, the sound of thunder or the sight of a garbage truck barreling around a corner—do something else that elicits a similarly uncomfortable response from her, but doesn't make her lose control. For example, if it's a noise issue, rhythmically tap a metal garbage-can lid on the pavement a few feet away from her while you have her in a sit-stay. Hold the leash so you can enforce these commands with an artful jerk. As she maintains her position, bring the lid closer.

If your dog is afraid of clanging noises, put her on a sit-stay, create the noise that bothers her, and correct her when she tries to bolt or shows other signs of anxiety. When she learns to concentrate on her obedience rather than her jitteriness, the fear will gradually evaporate.

As she learns to maintain the sit-stay despite this noise and proximity, up the ante by returning to the original distance, increasing the volume, and making the rhythm less predictable. Drag the lid behind her and even toss it into her field of vision so that it lands with a clatter. Again, move closer as she demonstrates her confidence.

Take the same approach if it's a particular stationary object that's making your dog crazy. Bring her as close as possible without inspiring a full-blown tantrum and begin practicing sit-stays. Once she's calm at that distance, move a little closer (using treats to bribe her, if she's receptive) and repeat. Continue moving closer until she's practically, or literally, on top of the object.

Practice these exercises every few days for a week or two. At that point, she should be desensitized enough to make this particular phobia a thing of the past. She may always acknowledge the object of her fear—any smart dog would do that—but she probably won't lose emotional control over it again.

Pulling on the Leash

Good leash manners are important for any hyper dog—except perhaps for a dog living in the middle of nowhere with a veterinarian who makes house calls, so that she'll never need to encounter another human being or domestic animal. Since that describes about three canines in all of North America, let's take a moment to recall how easy it is to achieve excellent leash etiquette.

While walking techniques such as weaving around poles can sometimes help, the Sneakaway is hands-down the easiest, most effective cure for pulling on the leash. There's no contest. Practice it diligently for a few sessions and your dog should be walking, standing, or sitting calmly at your side, her attention focused on your next move. Any time you sense that she's getting a bit sloppy, drop everything and do a few more Sneakaways to remind her who's driving this canine train.

Are you wondering if it's worth looking a little undignified? Well, consider how undignified you'd look getting dragged down the street with an armload of groceries or tumbling down a flight of stairs with thirty pounds of laundry spilling out to soften your fall. These are not situations in which you want your hyper dog to try to take control over your speed and direction; do your Sneakaways.

Backsliding or Untrained?

Is your dog really backsliding? Or is she simply untrained?

I'd been working with my first dog, Tess, at K-9 Obedience Training Club classes for seven months. She was advancing quickly, "graduating" from one level to the next, which was very exciting for a novice like me. She was so good, in fact, that I jumped at the chance to take her to our first practice obedience match.

I was feeling quite proud and confident when we strolled into the park where the match was being held—strolled in, and suddenly found ourselves surrounded by hundreds of barking dogs and frantic owners. Tess did what dogs do their first time in such a situation: She acted like she hadn't had even an hour of training. She wouldn't sit, she wouldn't stay, she wouldn't heel. And she didn't even seem to care that she was being so uncooperative.

I, however, was thoroughly humbled. And after thinking hard about her poor showing, I realized that it wasn't a lack of cooperation on her part; she simply wasn't as thoroughly trained as I'd thought she was. Repetition alone doesn't ensure canine learning. Repetition in every different environment, under every conceivable distraction, is what does it.

Running Away

Running away seems to be one of those problems that can affect any dog, with no particular pattern. While your aging hyper Cocker Spaniel takes off down the road in pursuit of some doggy dream, your neighbor's bouncy young Corgi inexplicably hovers at her owner's side, waiting patiently for a break in the weeding that might mean a pat on the head or a word of praise.

What's the crazed owner of a canine escape artist to do?

First, it's essential that you teach your dog the "wait" command to prevent her from bolting out the door unleashed in the first place.

Second, work on the "come" command in the presence of increasingly irresistible distractions, until she responds reliably to a single word from you.

Third, learn how to get her to finish off these recalls, so that she is practically nuzzling you by the time she arrives—not dancing around just out of your reach. (See "Catch Me If You Can," page 208. And for a step-by-step primer on off-leash control, see the *Amiable Basics Handbook* and DVD, available at the www.dogclass.com online store.)

Finally, don't let what you perceive as peer pressure force you to unleash your dog before she's 100 percent reliable. If you can't help but feel competitive with other dog owners, then let that be your motivation for sticking to your training program.

To give your dog a little freedom without compromising her safety, keep her on a 50-foot light line.

That way, you'll be able to enforce the "come" command even if she hasn't yet perfected her obedience to it.

Obey Refuses To

A classically manic hyper dog, my young Rat Terrier, Obey, usually does a few things exceptionally well—one of them being to stay close to me in the courtyard that serves as her toileting area, even when I've dropped her leash to let her sniff to her heart's content.

That all changed recently when my boyfriend took Obey out for me, dropped her leash, and watched helplessly as she pivoted and dashed off to the nearby parking lot. He set off in a panicky pursuit, only to find her busily greeting a neighbor whose distinctive voice apparently fascinates her.

He mentioned the episode but I wasn't concerned. Or at least I wasn't concerned until I took her out to the courtyard the next day, dropped her leash as usual, and watched in shock as she repeated her new disappearing act for me.

Recovering quickly, I said "eh eh" as jarringly as I could. It's a sound that usually stops her in her tracks, but not this time. She headed straight for the parking lot and proceeded to tear around it, apparently in search of her new friend.

I was able to retrieve her in almost no time, but her behavior made me uneasy. So it's with some embarrassment that I admit it happened a third time.

We're now in recovery, Obey and I. I often take her out on a light line. It gives her plenty of opportunity to take off—and gives me plenty of opportunity to do Sneakaways or enforce commands in response, thereby refocusing her attention on me.

We'll continue this work until I can once again stop her in the midst of a dead run away from me with a single word. Only when I've regained one-command control over her will I once again trust her on a dropped leash.

Scratching

See Digging.

Stealing

Have you ever left a loaf of bread sitting perilously close to the edge of a counter, within millimeters of a hungry hyper dog's nose? Tossed a wallet carelessly onto an end table before heading upstairs to shower and change? Left a well-worn journal sitting on the coffee table after adding a final entry?

. . . always on the prowl for a snack.

Some dogs are natural-born kleptomaniacs . . .

Fortunately, you can suppress that tendency with a well-timed shaker can hitting the dog's back end. Don't worry about hurting her; you won't.

If so, then you may already be well aware that your dog has no qualms about taking what doesn't belong to her and devouring or destroying it. And you'd probably like to keep it from happening again.

Unfortunately, this thievery is not something that can be entirely trained out of a klepto-inclined dog. It's true that if you catch her in the act, you can correct her with a quick jerk of the collar or a spritz of Bitter Apple on the lipline. And if you discover a theft after the fact, you can leash her and invite her to do it again—and then correct her with a jerk or a spritz if she takes you up on the offer. These efforts may, in the long run, help her resist all but the most powerful temptations.

Feeling a Little Smug?

Beware! Overconfidence on the part of a hyper dog owner has led to more destruction, anguish, and heartache than most of us experienced in our teens.

At a local trade show not long ago, I ran into the owners of a six-month old Labrador Retriever, a recent graduate of our puppy class. They were delighted to tell me that Buck had also just graduated from his crate and that he was now spending his time roaming free in their home.

"Oh oh," I thought, although I didn't say anything. Maybe I was just being paranoid. Maybe the pup was whiling away the hours with a good long nap and a little window gazing.

That was in the morning. I ran into them again in the afternoon, and saw immediately that the happy glows they'd worn just a few hours earlier had totally disappeared.

I asked what was wrong.

"Oh," said the wife tearfully, "Bob went home at lunch to take Buck out, and. . . ." She stopped, unable to continue.

Bob finished for her. "And I discovered that he had eaten the arm off my new Italian leather recliner." He tried to smile gamely, as if he'd just encountered an amusing little dip in the road to perfect obedience. But he looked sick.

"I guess he wasn't quite ready for that much freedom," I said, not knowing what else to offer.

"Guess not," he agreed.

The moral of this story is clear: Be stingy about giving your dog freedom. Assume that you've just been lucky so far and that the other shoe is about to drop. Make her earn her freedom in small increments, starting with rooms where she really can't do too much damage. And if she shows she can't handle the responsibility, return immediately to confining her when you can't be there to supervise her.

Otherwise, prevention is the key. Keep out of her reach everything she'd be even mildly interested in possessing, from garbage to laundry, hairbrushes to DVDs. When you're home, keep your eyes on her or umbilical cord her; when you're not, confine her to a dog-proofed room or her crate. Teach her the "drop it" command, and enforce it every time she picks up something that doesn't belong to her.

Whining

See Barking and Baying.

Zoning Out

Ever find your hyper dog spacing out on you—apparently not listening to you, or looking at you as if she'd never heard the command before, or perhaps not paying any attention to you at all as she pursues more interesting sights, smells, or sounds?

Chances are she's not being stupid, stubborn, or spiteful. She's just being forgetful or inattentive, and it's likely that she hasn't learned the command as solidly as you thought she had.

Don't repeat the command; that will only teach her that it's okay to ignore you. And don't bother yelling at her; it won't improve her response *or* understanding. Instead, quickly and firmly enforce the command, giving her lots of praise and using the appropriate body language.

For example, if she has ignored your command to come, you might walk up to her, jerk her collar toward you, and then briskly back or run away from her, saying, "good good good good GOOD!" Then, as she arrives, squat down and keep your hands in to receive her snuggles or kisses.

In other cases, you might need to apply remedial training, going back to square one for the command at issue. In this example, you'd put a leash on her, set her up with a distraction, then call "come" and deliver an instant jerk as you back away and praise her.

And in a worst-case scenario, where she not only ignores your initial command but continues ignoring you even after you've leashed her, you'd want to go back to the basics, including plenty of Sneakaways executed on a fifteen-foot longe line.

CITY DOG, COUNTRY DOG

No matter where you live with your dog, your surroundings will present special challenges—and extra opportunities. You can and should have a well-mannered dog anywhere you live. Your neighbors will thank you.

City Challenges

City dwellers face a number of unique challenges in raising hyper dogs. Perhaps the most obvious is the sheer volume of everything—people, dogs, cats, traffic, noises, smells, stairs, elevators, bikes, wheelchairs, towering structures, metal gratings in the pavement, flag-festooned festivals, drunk partiers, and not a whole lot of room to burn off their energy.

On the one hand, you want your hyper dog to take kindly to all these people, places, and things, so she can enjoy the mental stimulation and emotional highs of interacting with lots of different people and dogs. On the other hand, you want her to have a fear of some of them—

especially the exteriors of cars, vans, and trucks on the move. And above all, you need her to have a healthy respect for you and whatever commands you give her.

In all cases, the solution is solid obedience training.

For me and my hyper dogs, every step of every outing is a chance to practice obedience. When I am unlocking my bike or taking out garbage, carrying in groceries or lugging around laundry, we are always practicing tasks such as sit-stays and heeling on a loose leash. And in fact, one of the best things about city living is the wealth of distractions that are readily available—distractions that can be used to teach our hyper dogs to obey us no matter what temptations may arise. Training amid distractions is absolutely crucial to achieving one-command control, and if you live in the city, you won't have to go far to find them.

There are drawbacks to owning a dog of any temperament in the city, of course. To deal with them, you'll need to be vigilant. For instance:

- You have to be on the alert at all times, keeping an eye out for everything from traffic to creatures, human and otherwise, who would do your dog harm.
- You have to make sure your dog is properly socialized, so she's never a threat to others.
- For your own safety when you're carrying loads up and down stairs, you need her to walk politely on a slack leash.
- Because of the volume of sensory data bombarding us in urban areas, you may need to put more time into combatting phobias, which may be slightly more prevalent in city dogs.

Still, a hyper dog—one who's eager to share your urban experiences—is the perfect companion for a city dweller.

Suburban Snags

If you're a hyper dog owner living in the suburbs, you have your own canine issues to deal with. One of the more difficult ones can be excitement bordering on aggression when guests arrive. Suburban dogs just aren't all that used to this sort of event. They can become either territorial or—more likely with a hyper dog—so overwhelmed with joy and hospitality that their welcoming leaps become dangerous to anyone who gets in the way.

The immediate fix is to enforce a series of Rapid-fire Commands or, if you have the space, Sneakaways. Either technique will help you get her focused on you.

As a long-term solution, you'll need both obedience training and a bold plan of socialization to desensitize her to other people. Begin by setting her up with the help of some friends posing as guests. Your goal is to correct her repeatedly until she relaxes and stands at your side on a slack leash. As a variation, work on getting her to stand quietly on the

Wait!

If your dog loves to charge through open doors when company arrives or when you're trying to enter with an armload of groceries, there's a simple solution: the "wait" command, enforced by giving her the impression that the door is snapping at her nose each time she attempts to slip over the threshold uninvited.

To teach it, rush up to a closed door, tell her "wait," and open the door wide enough to be inviting but not so wide that she could charge through unimpeded—eight to sixteen inches, say. Don't let go of the handle. The moment she pokes her nose into the opening, tap the door on it, quickly enough that she backs off. (*Never* close the door completely when making this correction!) After the tap, immediately open the door enough to give her the opportunity to try again; if she does, repeat the correction. If she doesn't, open the door a little bit more and repeat the correction as needed.

Once she's begun hanging back a bit, even in the presence of an open door, create some new temptation on the other side of the door—food, for instance. Repeat the nose bumping as needed.

Finally, stand on the other side of the door so that she can't see you, leave it open a crack, and bump her nose as soon as it appears. Add a temptation once again and repeat.

Repeat this entire exercise at each of the entrances to your house, as well as at various interior doors. Then start walking through the door yourself while she hangs back and waits, just as you've commanded. It shouldn't take long for her to respond beautifully at any door—and even in situations where there's no door, such as between two rooms or at the end of your driveway when you're headed for the mailbox. When you're ready, release her with a "chin-touch okay."

Note that "wait" is not the same as "stay." "Wait" means "don't cross this line," not "don't change your position." If you tell your dog to wait in the kitchen while you step into the dining room, she will be free to move about wherever she wants as long as she doesn't follow you into the dining room. If you tell her to stay, on the other hand, you're telling her not to move.

front steps or porch when guests arrive, using the Magic Marker trick. Or, if she's a small dog, add platform training to the mix.

A somewhat related problem is aggression on the part of a fenced-in hyper dog. This aggression is normally expressed by snarling, biting, and lunging at passing people or animals—sometimes so determinedly that the dog manages to force her way under, over, or even through the fence.

Sometimes it's almost understandable. For instance, your dog's behavior may be a reaction to neighbor kids deliberately harassing her or to a stray dog looking for a fence fight. But if someone ends up getting hurt, the blame will land squarely on your dog's shoulders—and on yours. A good owner simply has to prevent such a dog from responding aggressively.

Rapid-fire Commands may not work in this situation. Instead, keep a long line attached to her collar while she's outside and a bottle of Bitter Apple within easy reach. Then, as soon as she starts charging or snarling, dash over to her and apply Bitter Apple to her lip line. Repeat whenever necessary until she ignores her tormenters.

Country Challenges

On the surface, it would seem that country living is ideal for a hyper dog—lots of room to run, a toilet at every tree, no neighborhood children to pester her, and no neighbors to complain about her barking. But as anyone who has owned a hyper dog in the country will tell you, the reality is not quite as rosy as it looks on paper.

Housetraining, for instance, is not simply a matter of opening the door and sending your dog out to train herself. Although I know how tempting it is to try this (and, as I said earlier, gave in to the temptation myself with one of my first dogs), it's a big mistake. With all the distractions out there, she's likely to chase around sniffing everything in sight, forgetting all about the "potty outside" you mentioned when you let her out. And she's likely to remember that purpose only later, when she's back inside with nothing to distract her.

The answer, of course, is to housetrain the hyper country dog just as we do hyper city and suburban dogs.

Another problem country owners can run into involves a hyper dog's effusive greeting of the relatively rare visitor who dares to pull into the driveway—a greeting that can involve barking, slobbering, and jumping up on the driver's door.

In many cases, this is a job for Sneakaways. You might not want to wait for the next unsuspecting visitor to arrive; instead, put her on a longe line and set her up by getting a friend to pull his car into your driveway, over and over again. Each time she heads for the car, pivot and head in the opposite direction just as quickly as you can.

WELCOME TO MY WORLD

Barb Pierce, an instructor of ours who's now in her 70s, recently sent me a note about the impact her new hyper dog, Dottie, has had on her life. Here's part of her letter:

> I've also become neater about my house. She notices all changes—a blanket on the couch, a pair of shoes on the floor, etc. Small things like shoes, she grabs and runs past me to show me that she has them, then tries to make a game of it. Thank goodness we learned "drop it" fairly early in our classes!
>
> I no longer have uncovered wastebaskets in my house, because she empties them. I don't leave mail, books, or magazines laying around on low tables anymore, either.
>
> I used mousetraps to break her of taking toilet paper off the roll and running with it. But when she learns an acceptable behavior like ignoring the toilet paper, she is quick to move on to another, less acceptable behavior!
>
> I have learned NEVER to put down any knitting or sewing and leave the room.
>
> So she does keep me alert. I guess what I hoped when I bought her is that she would keep me young, and she's certainly trying to do her job! Though she is rather exasperating at times, I'm not the least bit sorry that I got her, and think I'd be rather bored with a really laid-back dog.

Border Collie Dottie really keeps Barb Pierce on her toes. But, like other hyper dog owners, Barb doesn't seem to mind. In fact, she claims she'd be bored with a more laid-back canine companion.

Some people like high-maintenance relationships, lifestyles, vehicles, you name it. I don't understand any of these things; keep it simple for me.

But, like Barb, I suspect that I'd be rather bored with a laid-back dog. It would be like eating boiled hamburger or plain oatmeal—nourishing but not at all exciting.

Hyper dogs are more like sushi or baklava—complex, exotic, endlessly interesting. They are deep and intelligent and their hyperness can be harnessed and guided in all kinds of wonderful directions.

Why would you settle for anything less?

Index

About the Authors

....

Amy Ammen is among the nation's foremost authorities on training unusual breeds and solving difficult, confounding, and potentially life-threatening problems. She launched her own multi-campus school, Amiable Dog Training, 25 years ago in greater Milwaukee; in the years since, she and her staff have trained tens of thousands of dogs.

Amy hosts *Your Family Pet*, a weekly radio show on WRRD-AM 540 in Milwaukee, regularly appears on television to give advice about dogs, and is frequently quoted in print. Her dancing dogs are headliners at some of Wisconsin's most popular family-friendly festivals; a primary purpose of these performances is to educate young people about dog safety and how to be a dog's best friend. She also conducts seminars for dog clubs nationwide.

Amy has shared her expertise and experiences in five previous books: *Dual Ring Dog, Training in No Time, Dog Training: Your Happy Healthy Pet, The Everything Dog Book* and *The Everything Puppy Book*. She has also written dozens of articles in canine publications, ranging from *Dog Fancy* to *AKC Gazette*. She has produced a series of DVDs as well.

This is her first write-from-scratch book with **Kitty Foth-Regner**, a Waukesha, Wisconsin, freelance copywriter who has edited text for Amy over the years between marketing-communications assignments.

The author of scores of business-to-business brochures, articles, white papers, scripts, and direct-mail campaigns, as well as a 1987 medical thriller, *The Cure*, Kitty is also a pushover dog owner. She first sought Amy's help back in 1987, desperate for a way to stop her first Bassett Hound from dismembering every book and leather item in the house. Basic training principles and the strategic use of Bitter Apple provided the needed relief in a matter of days, and not so incidentally sparked a friendship that has weathered many years and many canine calamities.

Amy and Kitty came up with the idea for this book a couple of years ago when Kitty, apparently forgetting the reason they met in the first place, was complaining that her current dogs were so much more *hyper* than her idyllic creatures from the late 1980s.

"They're not just hyper," Amy said, laughing. "They need more direction. Perhaps we should revisit those old 'magical' procedures."

She was right. And as they started going over ideas for a program to turn Kitty's hyper dogs into contented canines with impeccable manners, this book was born.

Amy Ammen (seated) and Kitty Foth-Regner, with (left to right) Shadow, Able, Lucy, and Obey.

Photo Credits

....

PRAISE FOR *HIP IDEAS FOR HYPER DOGS*

The book covers a multitude of wonderful ideas and ways to solve behavior problems in dogs. Amy's methods of training reflect enjoyment for both handler and dog.

—Patricia Krause, retired assistant vice president of companion events, American Kennel Club

Amy Ammen and Kitty Foth-Regner have put together a wealth of information that will be a valued resource for anyone with a hyper dog. I don't know of any other resource that so clearly describes such a broad spectrum of activities to channel a dog with boundless energy.

—Gary Wilkes, creator of Click and Treat™ training